Domesday Heritage

TERRA SCE MARIE GLASTINGBERIENSIS.

Ecclia Glastingberie habet in ipsa uilla xii. hid q̄ nunq̄ geldauit. Tra e xx. car. De ea st in dnio x. hide 7 dimid uirg mi. Ibi. v. car. 7 xii. serui. 7 xxi. uilli. 7 xxxiii. bord cu. v. car. Ibi. cu. fabri. 7 iii. arpenz uinee. 7 lx. ac tra. 7 cc. ac pasture. 7 xx. ac silue. 7 ccc. ac silue minute. Valet xx. lib.

Huic æcclæ aduert insula q̄ uocat Mere. Ibi st lx. ac tre. Tra. i. car. q̄ ibi e. 7 x. piscatores. 7 iii. piscarie redd. xx. den. 7 vi. ac tra. 7 ii. arpenz uinee. Valet xx. solid.

Alia insula p an ibi q̄ uocat Wadeberie. Ibi st vi. ac tre. 7 iii. arpenz uinee. Valet iiii. solid.

Tercia insula adiacet ibi 7 uocat Bereuesie. In qua st ii. hide q̄ nunq̄ geldauit. Ibi e. i. car. cu. i. bord. 7 ii. ac pa. 7 una ac silue minute. Valet xv. solid. Godum ten de abbe.

Ipsa æcclia ten Winescote. T.R.E. geldb p. xv. hid. Tra e. xxx. car. De ea st in dnio. v. hide una 7 dim. Ibi. ii. car. 7 iii. serui. 7 xx xiiii. uilli. 7 vi. bord cu. x. car. Ibi molin redd. v. solid. 7 lx. ac pa. 7 una leu pasture in lg 7 lat. Silua. ii. leu lg. 7 una leu lat.

De hac eadê hui ten de abbe Rogeri. ii. hid. 7 dim. Radulf? i. hid. 7 pbr. e. p̄pe dim hid. Ibi st v. car. Hoc totu ualet abbti. viii. lib. hoib3 eis. lv. solid.

De tra hui ten epis ēstantiens de rege. i. hid. 7 uat. xx. solid. Brictic lib tenuit T.R.E. sed ñ poterat ab eccla separari.

Ipsa æcclia ten Middeltone. T.R.E. geldb p. vi. hid. Tra e. vi. car. De ea st in dnio. iii. hide. 7 vii. ac. 7 ibi. ii. car. 7 viii. uilli. 7 i. bord. cu. iiii. car. Ibi. l. ac pa. 7 c. ac pasture. Valuit 7 uat vi. lib.

Rogeri ten de eccla Lidefort. Aluuard tenuit T.R.E. nec pot p̄t ab eccla separari. 7 geldb. p. iiii. hid. Tra e. v. car. De ea st in dnio. iii. hide. 7 dimid uirg. 7 ibi. ii. car. 7 vi. serui. 7 vi. uilli. 7 iii. bord cu. i. car 7 dim. Ibi molin redd. xx. solid. 7 xl. ac pa. Valuit 7 uat. iiii. lib.

Ipsa æcclia ten Sapesuuich. T.R.E. geldb p xxx. hid. Tra e. xl. car. P̄t hanc te abb tra. xx. car. q̄ nunq̄. geldt. Ibi st. xii. car. 7 alibi. iiii. car in dnio. 7 vi. serui. 7 v. colibri. 7 xv. uilli. 7 xii. bord. Ibi lx. ac pa. 7 lx. ac pasture. 7 lcu. ac silue minute.

De his xxx. hid ten Rogeri de abbe. v. hid in Sutone. 7 v. hid in Leduuintone. 7 v. hid in Cepcone. 7 v. hid in Caldecote. Hi st teneb. xiiii. tain T.R.E. 7 ñ poterant ab eccla separari. Ibi st in dnio. x. car. 7 xi. serui. 7 xix. uilli. 7 xxii. bord cu. viii. car 7 dim. Ibi. c. ac pa. una m̄ xxxi. ac silue minute.

De ast xxx. hid ten Aluued. v. hid in Hunlauintone. Ibi ho ii. car. Ibi. v. serui. 7 xii. uilli. 7 viii. bord cu. vi. car. Ual x. sot. De ead tra ten Warmund. hid de abbe. Ibi st. i. car. iiii. bord. Hoc totu ualet abbti. xii. lib. Rogerio. xxv. lib. Aluuedo. vii. lib.

Ipsa æcclia ten Soure. T.R.E. geldb p. xii. hid. Tra e. xx. car. De ea st in dnio. v. hide. 7 ibi. ii. car. 7 ii. serui. 7 xii. colibri. 7 xxv. uilli. 7 xii. bord. cu. xiii. car. Ibi. xxx. ac pa. 7 xii. ac silue minute. Valuit. x. lib. Modo. xxiiii. lib.

Walteri ten de abbe Cosintone. Aluuin tenuit de abbe T.R.E. 7 geldb. p. iii. hid. Tra e. vi. car. De ea e in dnio. i. hida 7 ibi. ii. car. 7 iii. serui. 7 xx. uilli. 7 xv. bord cu. v. car. Ibi. x. ac pa. 7 ii. ac silue minute. Valuit 7 uat. vi. lib.

Rogeri ten de abbe Bereberge. Osuuald tenuit de abbe T.R.E. 7 geldb. p. ii. hid. Tra e. iii. car. Ibi st. iii. uilli. 7 ii. bord cu. ii. car. 7 in dnio dimid car. 7 xii. ac pa. 7 xx. ac pasture. Valuit. xxx. solid Cu recep. xl. solid uat.

Aluuicre ten de abbe Blachefort. Alnod tenuit de abbe T.R.E. 7 geldb. p. iiii. hid. Tra e. vi. car. In dnio st. iii. car. 7 v. serui. 7 xii. uilli. 7 x. bord cu. iiii. car. Ibi. xxx. ac pa. 7 xl. iii. de pasture. 7 xl. vii. ac silue. Valet. c. sot.

Godescal ten de abbe Bruuelle. Aluuard tenuit T.R.E. geldb p. ii. hida 7 dimid. Tra e. iiii. car 7 dim. In dnio e. i. car. 7 ii. serui. 7 iii. bord cu. i. car. 7 xxv. ac pa. Valet xl. sot. Xdo recep: v. solid.

Ipsa æccla ten Walrone. T.R.E. geldb p. xxx. hid. Tra e. xl. car. De ea st in dnio. xx. hide. 7 iiii. car. 7 iiii. serui. 7 xxii. uilli. 7 xii. bord cu. xviii. car. Ibi. l. ac pa. pastura. xii. q̄ lg. 7 una q̄ lat. Silua. cii. q̄ lg. 7 iii. q̄ lat. Valet abbi. xxx. lib.

De his. xxx. hid ten de abbe Rogerus. v. hid in Contone. Walteri. iii. hid in Lissecore. 7 iii. hid in Pecuuelle. Qui teneb T.R.E. ñ poterant ab eccla separari. In dnio st ibi. iii. car. 7 vi. serui. 7 xii. uilli 7 xii. bord cu. viii. car. Rogeri ho xx. ac tra. 7 vi. q̄ silue in lg. 7 una q̄ lat. Walteri. xii. ac pa. 7 xl. ac silue minute. Int eos ualet. viii. lib.

Rogeri ten de abbe Bodeslege. Winegod tenuit T.R.E. 7 geldb p. iii. v̄ge. Tra e. i. car 7 dim. q̄ ibi st cu. vii. bord. Ibi. vi. ac pa. 7 ii. ac silue. Valet x. solid.

Ide Ro. ten de abbe Donecase. Algar tenuit T.R.E. 7 geldb p. v. hid. Tra e. iii. car. De ea st in dnio. iii. hide 7 dim. 7 ii. car. Ibi. ii. car. 7 iii. serui. 7 v. uilli 7 x. bord cu. iii. car. Ibi. xl. ac pa. 7 x. ac silue. Valet. c. solid.

Ide Ro. ten de abbe Lissecore. 7 p̄t ad Walrone ptin̄ abbti. T.R.E. geldb p. ii. hid. Tra e. ii. car. Ibi st. ii. uilli 7 i. bord cu. i. car. 7 iii. ac pa. Valet. iiii. solid. xl. solid.

Girard ten de abbe Cranstone. Ulmer tenuit T.R.E. 7 geldb p. ii. hid 7 dim. Tra e. ii. car 7 dim. In dnio est. i. car. 7 v. serui. 7 ii. bord. ii. colibri cu. i. car. Ibi. xx. ac pa. 7 iii. ac silue. Valet 7 ualuit. l. solid.

Ipsa æccla ten Lega. T.R.E. geldb p. iii. hid. Tra e. x. car. De ea st in dnio. ii. hide. Una vex his fuit tainland. ñ tam poterat ab eccla separari. In dnio st. iiii. car. cu. i. serui. 7 vii. uilli 7 x. bord cu. v. car. Ibi. xxxv. ac pa. 7 xxx. ac pasture. 7 vi. ac silue. Valet. viii. lib.

Ipsa æccla ten Hame. T.R.E. geldb p xxvi. hid. Tra e. xx. car. De ea st in dnio. v. hide. 7 ii. car 7 dim. 7 ibi. iii. car. 7 v. serui. 7 xxi. uilli 7 xxi. bord cu. viii. car. Ibi. xxx. ac pa. 7 xvi. ac silue. Valet. xx. lib.

De hac tra hui ten de abbe Robt. i. hid 7 una v̄. 7 Serlo. v. hid. Girard. iii. v̄ge. Leuric 7 Aluuold 7 Almar tenuer T.R.E. nec poterant ab eccla separari. In dnio st. ii. car. 7 iii. serui. 7 ii. uilli 7 xiiii. bord cu. ii. car. Ibi. xxx. ac pa. 7 xx. ac pasture. Valet int tot. cx. solid.

Ipsa æccla ten Bodechelei. T.R.E. geldb p. xx. hid. Tra e. xx. car. De ea st in dnio. v. hide. 7 v. car. 7 vii. serui. 7 xx. uilli 7 vii. bord cu. vi. car. Ibi. l. ac pa. 7 c. ac silue. Valet abbi. x. lib.

De hac tra hui ten Turstin. viii. hid. Rogeri. ii. hid. Duo taini teneb de eccla T.R.E. 7 ñ poterant inde separari. In dnio st ibi. iii. car. 7 vi. serui. 7 xi. uilli 7 vi. bord cu. iii. car. Ibi. xiiii. ac pa. 7 xii. ac silue minute. Valuit 7 uat xvi. lib int eos. De ead tra ten Alestan de abbe. hid. Ibi st. i. car.

Hunfrid ten de rege. ii. hid in Loderforda. 7 p an huic to. Aluric teneb T.R.E. nec poterat ab eccla separari. Tra e. ii. car. Valet. xx. solid.

Ipsa æccla ten Pilcone. T.R.E. geldb p xx. hid. Tra e. xxx. car. P̄t hanc te abb tra de dim. xx. car. que nunq̄ geldau. In dnio st. x. car. 7 xx. serui. 7 xxi. uilli. xli. bord cu. x. car sup tra ñ geldant. Ibi. ii. molin redd. x. solid. 7 xl vi. ac pa. 7 xl. ac pasture. Silua. i. leu lg. 7 dim leu lat. De tra qn geldt ten Alnod monach. i. hid t ibali de abbe ecessu regis. t tainland fuit. 7 nec potest ab eccla separari. Tot ualet. xxiiii. lib. Valuit. xxii. lib.

De hac tra hui to ten Rogeri in Septone. iii. hid dimid. 7 in Coristone. iii. hid. Ulmer 7 Elmer te nuer T.R.E. 7 ñ poterant ab eccla separari.

Towns and villages of
Norman England
through 900 years

Domesday Heritage

ARROW BOOKS

Arrow Books Limited
62–65 Chandos Place, London WC2N 4NW

An imprint of Century Hutchinson Limited

London Melbourne Sydney Auckland Johannesburg
and agencies throughout the world

First published in 1986

Created and produced by PHOEBE PHILLIPS EDITIONS

Printed and bound in Great Britain by
Purnell and Sons (Book Production) Ltd, Paulton

ISBN 0 09 945800 4

Note: This book uses the pre-1974 counties, the closest approximation to counties at the time of *Domesday*.

Front cover: Brailles, Warwickshire

Frontispiece: *A page from* Domesday Book. *The parchment is slightly mottled here and there, and the ink has faded somewhat, but the neatly written text, with red lines for emphasis, is still clearly readable. Changes, erasures and marginal notes are used by historians to provide added information.*

Opposite page: *The* Domesday *volumes were stored in this chest in the 17th and 18th centuries.*

Contents

The Story of *Domesday Book*

Dr Elizabeth Hallam

Domesday Book, our earliest public record, is a rare and remarkable survey which details landholding and resources in late eleventh-century England. In its sophistication and in the comprehensiveness of its information, it remained unequalled until the nineteenth century, and the wealth of information it contains illuminates one of the most crucial times in our history: the conquest and settlement of England by William I and his Norman and northern French followers.

England in the eleventh century

The survey was essentially the product of the powerful will and relentless curiosity of William the Conqueror, but it could not have been made without the comparatively advanced administrative system that William inherited from his Anglo-Saxon predecessors.

By the year AD 1000, most of England was already divided into shires that remained more or less the same until the reorganization of our county boundaries in 1974. The pre-Conquest English kings exercised considerable authority, both in the Danelaw — those areas in East Anglia and other eastern and northern counties where Danish laws and customs had prevailed since the time of Alfred the Great — and in the other predominantly Anglo-Saxon regions. They were also powerful enough to gather substantial amounts of silver from the tax known as Danegeld, a name originally used in the 10th century for money raised to buy off marauding Danish armies. The silver was a sign of England's wealth, which was probably, even in this early period, founded in large measure upon its

Opposite page: *The ruins of Wigmore Castle in Herefordshire, set in an area that* Domesday *described as 'wasteland'.*

Below: *The* Domesday *volumes were put together from folded sheets of parchment, and then bound into substantial covers to protect them from damage.*

wool trade. With such resources and with the means for a ruler to tap them, England under Edward the Confessor was one of the greatest prizes in north-western Europe.

King Edward was childless, and although William, Duke of Normandy, was only related indirectly to him, Edward made him his heir in 1051. Powerful opposition came from Earl Godwin, the leading English noble, and his heir, Earl Harold. In January 1066 Edward died and Harold at once seized the throne. The new king was soon called upon to defend his realm against King Harold Hadrada of Norway. The Norwegians were decisively defeated and Hadrada slain, but less than three weeks later Harold was again fighting for his kingdom, against William of Normandy at Hastings. Harold's exhausted army, which had rushed down from the North in a forced march, was annihilated by the superior tactics of William's cavalry. This, the most momentous military event of English history, resulted eventually in the large-scale destruction of the English aristocracy, the imposition of an alien nobility and a Norman reordering of society along feudal lines.

William the Conqueror was one of the most able monarchs ever to rule England. He had succeeded to the ducal title in 1035 when still a child; by 1066 he had not only consolidated his power but extended its influence. After 1066 he dominated the politics of north-western Europe, having applied the same lessons of political realism taught him in the course of winning control of Normandy to the process of subjugating England.

Why the *Domesday* survey was made

During the last years of his reign William's power was threatened. The North was chronically rebellious, and in 1085, King Canute of Denmark and King Olaf of Norway gathered a great fleet of ships and made preparations for an invasion.

This did not materialize, but the cost of raising a defensive force may have suggested to the Conqueror the value of knowing, in as much detail as possible, precisely what his subjects possessed in England. *Domesday* was therefore created as a fiscal record, and as a detailed statement of lands held by the king and by his tenants, and of the resources which went with those lands. It recorded which manors rightfully belonged to which estates, thus ending years of confusion resulting from the gradual and sometimes violent dispossession of the Anglo-Saxons by their Norman conquerors. It was also a 'feudal' statement, giving the identities of the tenants-in-chief (land holders) who held their lands directly from the Crown, and of their tenants and under-tenants.

The compilation of such detailed information required a survey wholly unprecedented in its scope and precision. The fact that the scheme was executed and brought almost to complete fruition within two years is a tribute to the political power and formidable will of William the Conqueror.

How *Domesday Book* was made

One of the most important near-contemporary accounts of the making of the *Domesday* survey is that of the Anglo-Saxon chronicler. William, he said

had much thought and very deep discussion about this country – how it was occupied or with what sorts of people. Then he sent his men all over England into every shire and had them find out how many hundred hides there were in the shire,

LEDBURY, Herefordshire: *Detail of a Norman doorway in the minster. The church rivalled Hereford's cathedral in 1066, and Domesday records that a priest held half the hides, while military men held only one-fifth.*

or what land and cattle the king himself had in the country, or what dues he ought to have in twelve months from the shire. Also he had a record made of how much land his archbishops had, and his bishops and his abbots and his earls, and . . . what or how much everybody had who was occupying land in England, in land or cattle, and how much money it was worth. So very narrowly did he have it investigated, that there was no single hide nor a yard of land, nor indeed (it is a shame to relate but it seemed no shame to him to do) one ox nor one cow nor one pig which was there left out, and not put down in his record: and all these records were brought to him afterwards.

MUCH WENLOCK, Shropshire: *Interlaced arcading, a feature of the abbey's 12th-c. chapter house. The foundation had been started by St Milburga in the 8th c. and* Domesday *lists the village as being held by her church. See also page 59.*

This passage hints at the dismay and apprehension later expressed in the naming of the survey as *Domesday*, because of the association with the Day of Judgement, that terrible verdict against which there was no appeal.

Robert, Bishop of Hereford, was one of William's Norman followers. He wrote later that the king's men

made a survey of all England; of the lands in each of the counties; of the possessions of each of the magnates, their lands, their habitations, their men both bond and free, living in huts or with their own houses and lands; of ploughs, horses and other animals; of the services and payments due from each and every estate. After these investigators came others who were sent to unfamiliar counties to check the first description and to denounce any wrongdoers to the king. And the land was troubled with many calamities arising from the gathering of the royal taxes.

The survey was launched at William's Christmas court in 1085. Initially each tenant-in-chief, whether bishop, abbot or baron, and each sheriff and other local official was required to send in a list of manors and men. There were already earlier lists of lands and taxes in existence, which were drawn upon for the survey. All of England, apart from the northern counties, not yet firmly under Norman control, was divided into seven circuits. These circuits covered groupings of counties and to each of them were assigned three or four royal commissioners, high-ranking and trusted men whose task it was to test in the courts the accuracy of the information already provided.

The Worcester circuit, for example, was travelled by Remigius, Bishop of Lincoln, with a clerk and two monks in attendance, and three important laymen: Henry de Ferrers, Walter Giffard and Adam FitzHubert, brother of Eudo the Steward. One of the commissioners in the south-west was probably William, Bishop of Durham. These are the only names to have survived, but in their rank and status they were almost certainly typical.

It was the king's will that the survey should proceed swiftly, and we know that the initial stages were completed in 1086. The commissioners visited each of the county courts in turn and cross-questioned all those with an interest in the land, from the barons to the villagers. In *The Ely Inquest*, a contemporary document, even the questions they asked are cited:

They inquired what the manor was called; who held it at the time of King Edward; who holds it now; how many hides there are; how many ploughs in demesne (i.e., held by the lord) and how many belonging to the men; how many villagers; how many cottagers; how many slaves; how many freemen; how many sokemen; how much woodland; how much meadow; how much pasture; how many mills; how many fisheries; how much had been added to or taken away from the estate; what

LYDFORD, Devonshire: *One of 4 fortifications built by King Alfred in the 9th c. for defence against Danish marauders, Lydford was old at the time of* Domesday. *Its castle was a much-feared gaol for over 500 years, but today the village is almost a forgotten place.*

it used to be worth altogether; what it is worth now; and how much each freeman and sokeman had and has. All this was to be recorded thrice, namely as it was in the time of King Edward, as it was when King William gave it and as it is now. And it was also to be noted whether more could be taken than is now being taken.

The Ely Inquest also records the names of the jurors for some 'hundreds'. In Flendish Hundred, Cambridgeshire, they represented both the Norman and English races: Robert of Histon, Osmund the small, Fulcold a man of the Abbot of Ely, Baldwin the cook, Edwin the priest, Wulfric of Tevresham, Silac, and Godwin of Fulbourn.

The mass of evidence thus produced was written down in Latin—as was the survey as a whole—and this material was then sorted and re-sorted until it reached its final format under counties, landholders, hundreds or wapentakes, and manors.

One of the final circuit summaries has survived in the form of *Little Domesday* and perhaps a second in the Exeter (Exon) *Domesday*. The latter is something of a ragbag, containing records of the 1084–86 geld reassessment in the south-west, and the *Domesday* returns for Cornwall, Somerset, most of Devon, and parts of Wiltshire and Dorset, the rest having been lost. Arranged first by landholders and then by counties, it presents a great deal of information, and details of the livestock and the names of tenants often appear which were left out when the entries were transferred to *Domesday Book* itself.

Little Domesday and Great Domesday

Little Domesday Book is undoubtedly the final summary for the Eastern circuit, which consisted of Essex, Norfolk and Suffolk, some of the most populous counties of England. It is arranged by counties first and then by tenants. The work of several scribes, it is neatly if hurriedly written, the haste emerging in the many minor errors which appear in the text. The material for the three counties which it covers was never incorporated into the final summarized volume of *Great Domesday*, and this other volume was therefore preserved by the royal administration as part of the final record. Its headings were later picked out in red ink in order to give it a more formal appearance and to make it easier to find individual items amongst the mass of detail.

All the other final circuit summaries were recast into the more concise pattern of *Great Domesday*, almost certainly by one scribe, most probably based at Winchester. His task could well have been cut short—before he had time to incorporate the returns for the Eastern circuit, for London and for Winchester—by the death of William the Conqueror in September 1087. He has been tentatively identified as Sampson, a royal chaplain, later to become Bishop of Winchester. As he was confronted with the awe-inspiring challenge not merely of copying but of summarizing an enormous quantity of material as quickly as possible, it is hardly surprising that minor errors crept in and produced inconsistencies which have exercised *Domesday* scholars ever since.

Each shire summary was inscribed in a quire, that is, a small booklet, with 44 lines of script to each carefully ruled folio. The headings were all written in red, often in capital letters. As the scribe progressed, however, the writing became more compressed and relatively less neat and some of the county sections overlapped between quires. The summary of the final circuit to be dealt with, which covered

ELY, Cambridgeshire: *The west front of the cathedral. Originally a monastery (founded in 673), it was sacked by the Danes in 870, then rebuilt and, eventually, made a cathedral in 1109. The* Domesday *settlement was held by the Abbot of Ely.*

the West Midlands and the Welsh Marches, shows all the signs of having been dashed off extremely quickly.

Domesday is an impressive and agreeable document to consult and to handle. Throughout the centuries its custodians have treated it with great reverence, and its pages are for the most part in almost pristine condition. Because parchment benefits from the oil from human hands, the folios have remained soft and supple. The writing, which is in the Caroline minuscule style, is attractive and easy to read, although the Latin words are heavily abbreviated. In the early twelfth century the document was already known as a 'book', and it is probable that the quires were bound up at about that time. Recent research on the early covers of *Little Domesday* suggests that they date certainly from before 1220 and probably from far earlier than that.

ACTON BURNELL, Shropshire: *13th-c. castle. The village, held by Roger FitzCorbet in 1086, was made famous by Robert Burnell, Edward 1's Chancellor for 18 years from 1274.*

Domesday's two volumes were widely used for many centuries for administrative purposes. They are of equal if different value to the historian, the geographer, the archaeologist and the demographer of today.

Domesday Book in history

Most of *Domesday*'s detailed information went rapidly out of date, and subsequently the survey was to baffle and perplex medieval judges quite as much as later historians. But the *Book* remained as the proof of ancient landholding, rights

MONKTON, Kent: *Brass rubbing, a reminder that the village was held by the Archbishop of Canterbury's monks in 1086. Its Domesday entry lists a fishery and a salt-house as well as 2 churches.*

CHEPSTOW, Wales: *The ruins of the castle, built by William FitzOsbern, father of the 1086 holder, still command the skyline. The settlement appeared in the Domesday folios for Gloucestershire.*

and boundaries and this is a role which it has retained. It has been cited in court actions several times in the twentieth century and is still considered admissible legal evidence. Although until recently few have been appraised of its real contents, its reputation has remained resplendent down through the centuries. In the sixteenth century it began to be studied as a historical source, a process which continues unabated. The Victorians, with their English translations, gave it a new use and historical relevance.

Today *Domesday Book* is not just a relic of the past but a vital source book for understanding the origins of our modern institutions and society.

Inside the *Book*

Domesday Book can tell us a great deal about William's England. Feudal custom imposed on the English kingdom resulted in all land being deemed to be held from the king either directly or indirectly. The entries begin with the Crown lands, including those manors held directly by the monarch's tenants. The tenants-in-chief, great and small, were the next layer down in the feudal pyramid. In *Domesday Book* the ecclesiastics, the bishops and abbots, usually, but not invariably, come after the king. They are followed by the laymen; and the under-tenants of the tenants-in-chief, ecclesiastical and lay, are also named. Those who held the lands prior to the Norman seizure are always referred to as 'predecessors' of the current holders. King Harold is, except on two occasions which are clearly mistakes, consistently entitled 'Earl Harold'. Thus through these legal fictions was his reign consigned to oblivion.

The large-scale transfer of land had, not surprisingly, caused many problems, and there are numerous entries in *Domesday Book* that refer to disputes over rightful possession – indications that there was already much work for the lawyers.

Rents, tax and manorial values

The total value of the land in *Domesday* has been estimated at about £73,000 a year. Under-tenancies appear in abundance. Their holders generally owed military services to their lords, and those lords to the king. But there were also other ways by which land could be held. Most conspicuous in *Domesday Book* were leases or rents for money, and the figures for some of them were clearly exorbitant. The manor of Thaxted in Essex was worth £30 in 1066 and £50 in 1086, but its holder, Richard FitzGilbert, had leased it to an Englishman for an annual £60. His tenant had been unable to pay this inflated figure and had defaulted on at least £10 a year.

It used to be thought that the value which the *Domesday* commissioners assigned to any particular manor had no more than a general connection with its size. However, the manorial entries for Essex have recently been analysed by computer, with interesting results. When the total values are compared with the resources – such as the pasture, plough teams, mills and livestock – it soon becomes clear that in many cases a mathematical equation links the two: the commissioners were evidently instructed to assign a set value to each resource.

In some instances the values of the manors and their geld assessments are also connected. (These are the figures expressed in hides, which could be subdivided into four virgates; or in carucates, containing eight bovates; or in sulungs subdivided into four yokes; or in leets – according to the area of the country.) But that correspondence is far from invariable, because some districts, such as parts of Cambridgeshire, were assessed at favourably low levels, and some places were let off lightly or escaped altogether.

Comparison of the values of some manors in 1066 and 1086 shows that certain areas, particularly in northern England, had suffered terrible devastation in the interim. Cradwell in Yorkshire had a pre-Conquest value of 20s, but by the time of *Domesday* was worth only 5s 4d, and was uninhabited. It, like many others, had been ravaged by King William and his men, who had left a trail of devastation behind them. It was waste not in the sense of being uncultivable, but in that its value had been reduced. Harbury in Warwickshire had similarly been 'laid waste by the king's army' as it passed through. But the Conqueror was not the only person to blame for such problems. Raiders from Ireland, for example, had cut the value of

HEMSBY, Norfolk: *19th-c. farm cottage. Norfolk is one of the 3 counties in* Little Domesday Book, *and the surveyors often included details of livestock. The entry for Hemsby lists 160 sheep, a church and 2 salt-houses.*

West Portlemouth, a settlement near the South Devon coast, to a mere quarter of its earlier level.

Justice was also valuable business in the Middle Ages, and part of the profits of some manors came from the courts that were attached to them. In these cases, *Domesday* records that the yields of the soke (i.e. the jurisdiction) of a hundred or wapentake went to the holder of the manor. The king usually reserved two-thirds of the money made from justice in the shire or hundred court. The earl kept the rest, the third penny, which was usually paid to a particular manor.

To sum up, the so-called value of a manor was an estimate of the total its lord might receive annually in money and kind from his peasants, and would include, for example, a proportion of the eels caught or pigs kept, etc.

LITTLE DUNMOW, Essex: *Carved chair for the winners of the 'flitch' of bacon presented to any married couple who swear they have not regretted their marriage within the past year.* Domesday *Dunmow was divided between 7 landholders.*

The ordinary people of the manor

The life of most villages centred on the hall, where the court was held and where the lord often lived. Some of the halls had minor fortifications for protection. When a manor had more than one lord, it often had more than one hall; conversely when it had been leased to the peasants, it was sometimes said to have no hall. The reeve was the chief organizer of the manorial lands, and either worked for the lord or was elected by the peasants to act on their behalf.

The other leading man of the village was the priest. About a thousand are mentioned in *Domesday Book*, a mere fraction of the real total. Some priests had fat livings attached to their churches, but others were virtually indistinguishable from the villagers and joined in with the communal labour. Many, like Aelemaer, the pre-Conquest holder of Blofield in Norfolk, were married. There had been fresh legislation against clerical marriage in 1076 but it was to prove difficult to enforce.

The free peasants of the manor were known either as freemen or as sokemen. Distinctions between the two kinds are often very difficult to prove, and in many regions the two terms may have been used interchangeably. Free peasants are mentioned in all the counties, but by far the highest proportion was in the former Danelaw. It was long believed that the sokemen represent the descendants of the rank and file of the old Danish armies which had ravaged England two centuries before the Normans came. Compared with 1066, the numbers of freemen and sokemen in 1086 show a marked decline, suggesting that the Conquest had an adverse effect on men's liberty. Such individuals were free in their persons, but generally had obligations to their lord, including the obligation to attend his court.

The great majority of the *Domesday* peasantry, the villagers (villans), the smallholders (bordars) and the cottagers (cottars), were personally unfree. They had to render labour services to their lord, and they were tied to their manor, but they had a stake in its resources. The villagers accounted for about one-third of the total recorded population. Most were obliged to plough their lord's land as well as their own. At Leominster in Herefordshire they had to cultivate 125 acres in their lord's demesne (i.e., holding) and to sow it with wheat seed. At Pagham in Sussex they paid him one pig for every six that grazed the herbage, and at Wraxall in Dorset they gave him a rent of £3 a year. However, they might have substantial holdings of their own, and at Alverstoke in Hampshire they even held land directly from the Bishop of Winchester. The smallholders and the cottagers were lower down in the social scale. Their services to their lord were correspondingly greater than those of the villagers. The entry for Stokesay in Shropshire includes an

MONK'S RISBOROUGH, Buckinghamshire: *Medieval dovecote behind the church. The 1086 settlement was one of only 3 held in this county by the Archbishop of Canterbury.*

unusual mention of five female cottagers. At the bottom of the heap were the slaves, who were wholly unfree, the chattels of their lord, and who had no land. They numbered about one-tenth of the total recorded population, and were found predominantly in the south and west of the country. In 1086 they worked entirely for their lord, but the lot of their descendants gradually improved as they merged with the great mass of villeins. The freedmen (coliberts) of the south-western counties were already on that path.

Other members of manorial communities appear sporadically, some only in

LYME REGIS, Dorset: *The view from The Cobb, the port's curved, stone jetty. The structure is believed to have stood for more than 1000 years, and must surely have been used by 11th-c. fishermen, some of whom are mentioned in one of the resort's* Domesday *entries. See also page 56.*

certain regions. In counties bordering the Welsh Marches there are riders (radmen) and riding-men (radknights), who performed duties of escorting their lords, as at Ledbury in Herefordshire. *Drengs*, free peasants who held lands in return for military duties, are recorded in Lancashire and Yorkshire. Women are mentioned occasionally, such as the female slaves (*ancillae*) in West Midlands manors like Bishampton in Worcestershire. Dairymaids, nuns, widows and wives all make the occasional entrance, and at Barfreston in Kent there was one poor woman who paid 3¾d each year, for what is unknown.

England's population

Domesday Book is not a census. It records the heads of households but not necessarily the families which they supported. To attempt any calculation of the total population in England in 1086, therefore, some multiplier must be used, but slaves are probably recorded as individuals rather than as heads of families. Conversely, at least five per cent of the total population – such as retainers in castles, nuns and monks – is missing. Calculations for the missing areas in England must also be made and the Welsh areas excluded. A leading scholar has suggested that a multiplier of four would produce a total figure of a little under one and a quarter million, and a multiplier of five, about one and a half million. Other historians believe that two million would be more accurate.

All of these figures, however, show a marked decrease from the population estimates for Roman times. There may then have been as many as four million people, a figure not exceeded until about 1300.

The most densely populated areas, with more than ten people to the square mile, were parts of Lincolnshire, East Anglia and east Kent, with smaller concentrations in south Somerset and on parts of the South Coast. The whole of northern England, by contrast, together with the Weald, Dartmoor and the Welsh Marches, had less than three people to the square mile. Many places were not cultivable, others had been laid waste. For example, of 64 places which were attached to Preston in Lancashire, only 16 were inhabited, and those sparsely, but the actual number of people was unknown. The rest of the settlements were devastated.

BATTERSEA, Surrey: *Tower blocks on the south bank of the Thames. A valuable manor since 693, it was held by Westminster Abbey in 1086. Market gardens were started here at the end of the 16th c. by Huguenot refugees, and in the early 19th c. these lands supported an enormous herd of cows.*

The people of *Domesday*

Of the land described in *Domesday*'s 35 counties the king and his family held about 17 per cent, the bishops and abbots about 26 per cent, and the 190-odd lay tenants-in-chief held about 54 per cent. Some of the holdings were huge, and the dozen or so leading barons together controlled about a quarter of England. Such estates were often geographically scattered: 20 leading lay lords had lands in ten or more counties, and 14 had possessions both north of the Trent and south of the Thames. The dispersal was partly a matter of accident, but it did allow those whose possessions in the North were devastated to support themselves from the richer South.

In border areas, certain barons were granted compact estates in order to defend England against attack. For example, in 1071 the earldom of Chester was granted to Hugh 'the Fat' d'Avranches, who was to dominate the region for three decades whilst he waged bloody wars against the Welsh. His Cheshire lands listed in *Domesday Book* were worth only about £200 annually, but he had other estates in 20 shires valued at about £700, which enabled him to finance his conflicts.

The great majority of the *Domesday* landholders came from northern France, but there were still a few Anglo-Saxons and Danes. Only one member of the old nobility still possessed sizeable estates. Thorkell of Arden, who had lands in Warwickshire, had co-operated with the Conqueror and been permitted to inherit them from his father.

Many formerly independent Anglo-Saxon and Danish thanes and their descendants appear in *Domesday* as the under-tenants of Norman lords. One, a man called Toli, had retained a hold on his lands at Cowley in Oxfordshire which he had held freely before the Conquest. In 1086, however, he was the under-tenant of the Norman baron Miles Crispin. Another English under-tenant, Saewold, had kept property worth £10 in the same county, but it appears that he had problems in making ends meet, because he had mortgaged half of it to Robert d'Oilly. Such men were the sad remnant of a once proud and powerful aristocracy.

There was, however, one Englishman who occupied a place of the highest importance in 1086. He was the saintly Wulfstan, Bishop of Worcester. At first a monk, he rose to be schoolmaster, then prior, and in 1062, became bishop, an office he held until his death in 1095. Under him, the monks increased in numbers and zeal, and the cathedral school became and remained a centre of English learning. According to his biographer, Wulfstan was loved and respected by his community and by the people of his diocese alike.

Most of the high-ranking people cited in *Domesday* were men, but a few women do appear. Of these, the two most important were already dead in 1086. Queen Edith, Edward the Confessor's widow, had held estates worth £1600 each year, which after her death had reverted to the Crown. Matilda, William's queen, had similarly held valuable properties during her lifetime, and, although they appear in *Domesday* as Crown lands, their earlier ownership is made clear.

The most prominent living female in the survey was Judith, Countess of Northumbria and Huntingdon, who possessed substantial holdings and a dramatic past. A niece of William I, she had been married off to Waltheof, Earl of Northumbria, after William's conquest of the North. Waltheof was not at first seriously implicated in the 1075 rebellion, but, when Judith testified of his treachery to the king, he was cast into prison and was executed in 1076. Ten years later Judith held not only her dower, consisting of lands in Huntingdonshire, but also other manors which William the Conqueror had given her.

STAMFORD, Lincolnshire: *Stained glass in a medieval almshouse. Once the capital of the Fens, the town was held by 10 landholders at the time of* Domesday.

OTLEY, *West Riding, Yorkshire: A fragment of Saxon carving from the 9th-c. cross in the church. The settlement was held by the Archbishop of York before and after 1066, and a church is listed in its* Domesday *entry.*

The uses of the land: agriculture

In 1086, 80 per cent of the area cultivated in 1914 was already under the plough. About 35 per cent of the *Domesday* land was arable, 25 per cent was pasture and meadow, 15 per cent was woodland and the remaining area was occupied by settlements, by marginal land such as heath, moor and fen, and by devastated land. Such figures have been arrived at only by the most painstaking correlation of all available evidence.

The measurements for agricultural land are expressed in a variety of ways. The taxable units such as the hide and the carucate must originally have been linked to agricultural capabilities, but by 1086 were no more than arbitrary divisions. Another measurement given is that of ploughlands (land for x ploughs). On the face of it, this sounds like the amount of land which could support a given number of plough teams. However, there is frequently a puzzling discrepancy between the figures for ploughland and the – usually larger – actual number of ploughlands in a manor. The way in which figures for plough teams are recorded varies from region to region, and some authorities believe that these numbers, like the hide, represent units of fiscal assessment.

The figure giving the actual number of ploughs is the best guide to the agricultural capacity of the manor. A plough team consisted of eight oxen. Normally some teams were held by the lord and were worked for him, while others belonged to the peasants. Some areas, such as the Sussex coastal plain and parts of Herefordshire, were highly fertile and supported more than four plough teams to the square mile. At the opposite end of the scale were the poor lands, such as much of the North, the Somerset levels and Sherwood Forest, where there was on average one such team only to every two square miles or more.

The arable land was used to grow wheat, barley, oats and beans. The grain once produced had next to be milled to make flour. Some was ground by hand, but the 6000 mills which appear in *Domesday* must have coped with a high proportion of this heavy work. They were driven by water power: windmills did not appear in England for another century. Some *Domesday* mills were very lucrative, but others produced no rents; and fractions of mills, denoting multiple ownership, are not unusual. At Coleshill in Bedfordshire the three owners of the mill each took ten shillings from it. Sometimes a portion of a mill is missing from *Domesday Book*; at Leckford in Hampshire, half of one remains unaccounted for.

Gardens and orchards sometimes appear in the survey. Fruit, cabbages, peas, leeks, onions and herbs would have been grown in them. About 45 vineyards are also mentioned, and one at Wilcot in Wiltshire was said to be very productive.

Pasture, livestock and fisheries

Pasture was land where animals grazed all the year round. Meadow, which was much more valuable, was land bordering streams and rivers which was used both to produce hay and for grazing; the hay from Cogges in Oxfordshire produced a profit of 10s each year. Pasture was entered in *Domesday* less regularly than meadow, and, further to complicate matters, was measured in several different ways. In Essex, its size was estimated according to the number of sheep it could support; in Sussex and Surrey, sometimes according to the number of pigs. Linear dimensions or acreage are the units in the south-western counties.

Little Domesday and the Exeter (Exon) *Domesday* provide details of the livestock owned by the lord. We cannot, of course, know what proportion this was

of the total. Sheep were then, as later in the Middle Ages, of great economic importance. At Puddletown in Dorset, a large and complex manor, 1600 sheep are mentioned. Other animals in the records are goats (used to produce milk), cows, oxen and horses – including packhorses, wild horses and forest mares. Bees, extremely important as the producers of honey and wax, were frequently mentioned, as at Methwold in Norfolk, where there were 27 hives. In some areas the total number of animals is given, in others only the proportion due to the manor, which was typically one pig in seven.

Inland and coastal fisheries recur throughout *Domesday Book*. Many of the references are to weirs along the main rivers, but fishponds, as at Sharnbrook in Bedfordshire, are also noted. A millpond at Stratford in Warwickshire is said to have produced 1000 eels each year. Petersham in Surrey rendered 1000 eels and 1000 lampreys.

HAXEY, Lincolnshire: *Strip farming is a form of cultivation that goes back to* Domesday, *when the low ridge of clay – the Isle of Axholme – on which the village stands was surrounded by waterlogged, flat land.*

Salt-making, mines and quarries

Not all the unfree people who appear in the *Domesday* survey worked on the land. There are some references to localized industrial activity, although these are far from comprehensive. Salt, which was essential for the preservation of food, was produced by the evaporation of brine from the sea and river estuaries or from inland saline springs. There were two inland centres, Droitwich in Worcestershire; and Northwich, Middlewich and Nantwich in Cheshire. Salt-making in Worcestershire was flourishing in the late eleventh century. Droitwich alone, it was said, had 263 1/2 salt-pans and there were others nearby. Lead vats, furnaces and cartloads of wood for fuel also found an incidental mention. The Cheshire salt industry had by contrast apparently fallen on hard times. When Earl Hugh arrived in the area, only one salt-pan was still in operation. By 1086 a minor recovery seems to have occurred, but the value of the pans combined was only one-third of

HARMONDSWORTH, Middlesex: *The interior of the great tithe barn, built in 1426, recalls the impressive solemnity of a church or abbey. The real, partly 12th-c. church, on the site of the one mentioned in* Domesday, *is the village's oldest building.*

the 1066 total. On the coasts, salt-making was undertaken on a smaller scale.

The extracting and forging of iron was widespread in eleventh-century England (though less so than in Roman times). Iron mines are mentioned in the Rhuddlan entry, and the city of Gloucester is said to render iron – presumably mined in the forest of Dean – for the king's ships. Lead-working is mentioned only in Derbyshire, where, for example, Wirksworth is said to have three mines and Matlock Bridge one. In 1066, the people of Bakewell, Ashford and Hope had rendered money, honey and five cartloads of lead, each of 50 slabs, but by 1086 a money rent alone was paid. Quarries appear in seven places – among them Limpsfield in Surrey and Whatton in Nottinghamshire – and there are three potteries, one of these at Westbury in Wiltshire. But such activities normally lie outside *Domesday*'s terms of reference and are mentioned only incidentally.

WHATTON, Nottinghamshire: *Late 13th-c. carved bracket in the church. Unusually, the* Domesday *entry lists a millstone quarry.*

Woods, forests and game-parks

Although large areas of woodland were rare, smaller woods, used for timber, for brushwood and for pasturing swine, were a vital part of the manorial economy, and were scattered fairly widely throughout the country. In some regions they were measured in *Domesday* according to the number of pigs which they could support, in others by their actual size. Underwood or coppice occurs frequently and sometimes the kinds of tree – alder, ash, oak, thorns and willow – are given. There are a number of specific mentions of assarting (clearing the wood for agricultural purposes). Despite the tremendous effort involved it was probably a widespread practice.

Royal forests had since Anglo-Saxon times been areas used for the king's hunting. The Conqueror, whose attachment to the chase is well known, imposed harsh laws in his forests to protect the game, and particularly the deer and wild boar. Forests were not necessarily woodland areas, many having substantial proportions of open land within their boundaries. The New Forest, which occupies its own section of the Hampshire folios, is the only one specifically to be described in *Domesday Book*. Later chroniclers accused the king of having laid many villages waste to create it, but their assertions are not wholly borne out by the survey, which shows 40 settlements and even some agricultural activity within it. There are incidental references to land taken into the forest elsewhere, or to places devastated to make forest. Earl Hugh of Cheshire, like the king, had his own forest, later known as Delamere Forest. Such areas were administered by head foresters, who were trusted and sometimes powerful men. Waleran the Forester had substantial estates in southern England. In the forest of Essex, Robert Gernon took a swineherd from Writtle and promoted him to the lofty office of royal forester, a classic example of a man being raised from the dust.

The king, like other lords, had a number of enclosed parks for his game. A total of 35 of these 'parks for wild beasts' is mentioned in *Domesday*. There are also references to 'hays' or hedged enclosures in many forests, into which game was driven; Another popular aristocratic activity was hawking, and in many areas, hawks are noted as being paid as dues from individual manors. These birds were highly priced creatures: the entry for Worcester reveals that the citizens were obliged to produce either a Norwegian hawk each year or an extra £10 in rent.

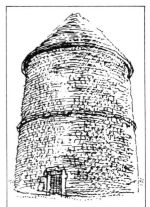

SIBTHORPE, Nottinghamshire: *Medieval dovecote with 1260 nesting places. The yew trees in the churchyard, said to be 1000 years old, would have been standing in 1086.*

Domesday Settlements Today

Villages, towns and hamlets listed in *Domesday Book* are as varied today as they were 900 years ago.

FORDINGBRIDGE, Hampshire: *Town on the River Avon.*

HINTON ADMIRAL, Hampshire: *Hamlet close to Christchurch. The Cat and the Fiddle is one of many attractive thatched pubs in Hampshire.*

SWAFFHAM PRIOR, Cambridgeshire: *Village with 2 churches in one churchyard. The ruined tower is Norman and Early English.*

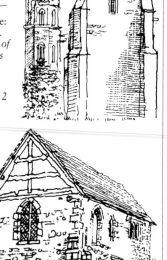

DONINGTON-LE-HEATH, Leicestershire: *Village with the county's oldest medieval house, built c. 1280.*

DUNWICH, Suffolk: *Parts of a cloister walk and refectory, all that remains of a Franciscan friary. Once the prosperous capital of East Anglia, the city was finally overwhelmed by the sea late in the 18th c., a fate foreshadowed in its Domesday description: 'Then 2 carucates of land, now 1. The sea carried away the other.'*

The *Domesday* boroughs

The treatment of boroughs is erratic. Many county sections begin with a description of the county town and other boroughs, but this is not a consistent pattern. London and Winchester are missing altogether, and, in some shire sections, the descriptions of boroughs come in the main body of the text. The entries vary from the long and disorganized to the brief and curt, suggesting that neither the commissioners nor the *Domesday* scribes were really sure how to incorporate them in the record. It is even possible that it was decided to include them only once the survey was already in progress. Nevertheless, there is much to learn from *Domesday Book* about urban life, customs and organization.

In a few cases there seems little obvious reason why a given place is called a borough. On the other hand, the descriptions of many show some or all of the characteristics which we would expect a borough to have in this period. These places first developed as fortified settlements. Trade was a crucial element and there were markets in many boroughs. The urban court and administration are also often mentioned in the *Book*; and for some towns, such as Shrewsbury, the legal customs are described. Before 1066 all boroughs had had one or more mints, and many still remained after the Norman Conquest. The moneyers who controlled them were wealthy and powerful people. In Lincoln they contributed £75 each year to the royal coffers.

The county towns were secure in their status as boroughs, but for others, particularly in parts of the south-west, their situation was less certain. Even in the largest towns, the burgesses often had interests in the fields outside and might well have taken part in their cultivation. Similarly, houses inside the town were frequently acquired by rural landholders, as well as by the Crown, which often had the controlling interest in urban property and affairs. The links between the towns and the countryside were thus very close.

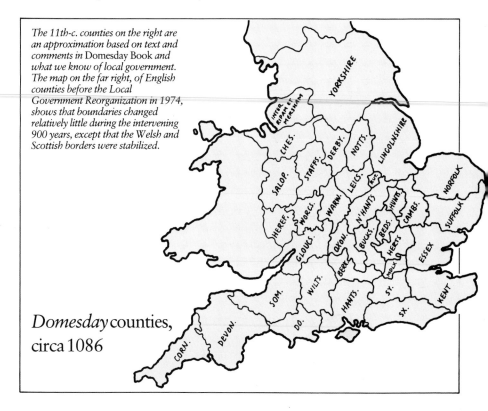

The 11th-c. counties on the right are an approximation based on text and comments in Domesday Book *and what we know of local government. The map on the far right, of English counties before the Local Government Reorganization in 1974, shows that boundaries changed relatively little during the intervening 900 years, except that the Welsh and Scottish borders were stabilized.*

Domesday counties, circa 1086

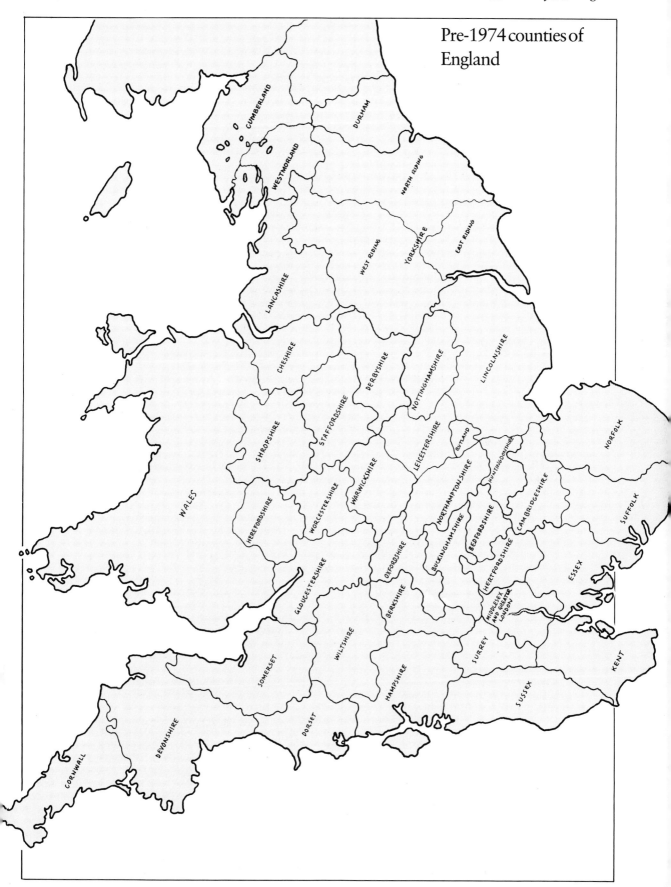

Pre-1974 counties of England

BRANSCOMBE, Devonshire:
*Church with a mainly Norman
transept. Aethelstan gave the
village to the Benedictine monks of
Exeter in the 10th c.*

ALTON, Hampshire: *Originally
Norman church. The settlement
was held by St Peter's, Winchester,
at the time of* Domesday.

Castles and churches

The few castles and churches built in the eleventh century but which still survive are a tangible link between the England of 900 years ago and the England of today. The White Tower at the Tower of London, constructed of white stone, remains a vivid reminder of William's dominance and authority. Most of the other castles of his day were built of wood but had a similar motte and bailey plan, of the kind illustrated on the Bayeux tapestry. *Domesday Book* mentions 48, scattered from Okehampton to Richmond, although other evidence suggests that there were many more. Some, such as Ewyas Harold in Herefordshire, had been built by

CASTLE RISING, Norfolk: *The
castle keep, one of Britain's most
elegant Norman remains. It was
built in c. 1150 by the son of
William the Conqueror's butler,
whose descendants, by the
maternal line, continued to preside
over local affairs until the 20th c.*

the Norman favourites of the Confessor, but the majority were post-Conquest, symbols of the new military order.

Parish churches constructed immediately after the Conquest were probably indistinguishable from those raised just before. They are not recorded systematically. Only 147 churches in Kent appear in the *Book* where other sources note at least 400. *Domesday* does give details about some of them. At Bermondsey there was a 'new and beautiful church'; at Old Byland there was one made out of wood; Netheravon church in Wiltshire was on the point of collapse. They are treated as potentially lucrative manorial appurtenances, and sometimes divided into fractions—as small as one-twelfth at Freekingham in Lincolnshire.

Castles and Churches in *Domesday* Settlements

Few churches and castles built in the 11th c. survive today in their entirety. However, by combining information in the *Domesday* entries with the physical evidence of Saxon and Norman artefacts, it is possible to trace the history of many buildings—or their sites—back to 1086 and even earlier.

FRAMINGHAM, Norfolk: *Church with a Saxon chancel and windows, on the site of the one mentioned in* Domesday.

KILPECK, Herefordshire: *Doorway of the church, which contains Saxon remains. The village was held by William FitzNorman who owned its castle, now in ruins.*

CONISBROUGH, West Riding, Yorkshire: *The castle keep, with 6 massive buttresses. Most Norman castles were built after 1066 and were originally made of wood.*

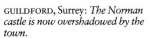

GUILDFORD, Surrey: *The Norman castle is now overshadowed by the town.*

HAMSEY, Sussex: *Medieval church with traces of 15th-c. paintings, probably on the site of the Domesday church.*

WARNFORD, Hampshire: *Norman church with 15th-c. benches and a Saxon sundial.*

HATHERLEIGH, Devonshire: Church of John the Baptist, noted for its 9th-c. Saxon font.

Some *Domesday* Settlements Then and Now

Although *Domesday Book* is essentially a census – of England's population and its resources – the text also reveals nuggets of information that give us a picture of the people and their concerns: Aelgar, who had enough land to live on from the Sheriff of Trent, so that she might teach his daughter gold embroidery; the Count of Mortain, who transferred a market from his manor of Launceston, in Cornwall, to his castle; and how makers of bad beer were punished with the dung stool in Huntingdonshire.

But above all, *Domesday* allows us to trace the history of more than 13,000 settlements from 1086 until today – 900 years during which some places grew into towns or cities, others fell into the sea, some were deserted, some dwindled to a single building.

The examples on the following pages have been specially selected to highlight aspects of this unique heritage. Entries are grouped alphabetically, and each section starts with a main entry which describes outstanding events – or people – in a settlement's history, introduced by its *Domesday* listing or listings. The short entries that follow start with the place's modern name in bold, followed by its pre-1974 county. The *Domesday* information is in italic, starting with the main landholders and under-tenants, separated with semi-colons if a place was divided into more than one holding. Thanes come at the end of a list of holders. More general information, including examples of dues such as eels rendered by tenants, completes the *Domesday* part of the entry. The modern or post-*Domesday* section is in normal type. 🏘 represents a village, ⛺ a small village or hamlet.

Translations of the *Domesday* entries, and the *Domesday* information, are from the Phillimore *Domesday Book* series: 35 volumes which correspond to the county divisions of the original.

Assessment in carucates for periodic tax used in northern and eastern England. 1 carucate equals 120 acres

Immigrant from France since the Conquest

Independent peasants who owed few dues to the manor, if any, but if called "sokeman", owed obligations, such as attendance at the manor court.

Modern name

1 bovate equals ⅛ carucate

1 sester equals about 32 ounces

Saxon holder, pre-1066

Tenant-in-chief

Peasant whose duties included military service (forerunner of a medieval knight)

About 1 acre

2 houses in Lincoln belong to the manor

Class of peasant with a cottage and little, or no, land

Rent which automatically increased if paid late

Autumn acorn and beech mast feed pigs

Before 1066

He could transfer his land to another tenant-in-chief

In ASHBY Edgar had 4 c. and 2 b. of land taxable. Land for 5 ploughs. Drogo has 2 ploughs there, and 2 Frenchmen and a man-at-arms have 2½ ploughs. 3 Freemen who render 2 sesters of honey. 2 cottagers. Vineyard, 1 arpent; pasture, 20 acres. 2 houses in the borough of Lincoln. Geoffrey has 60 acres of woodland for pannage there, for 10d of Warnod. Afric held it. He could go where he would. The value was £4, now 20s, found waste; tallage 10s. The full jurisdiction belongs to Botford.

Law cases involving inhabitants of Ashby were tried at Botford, whose lord kept the fines

Was either uncultivated or unusable when the Norman tenant acquired the manor

Common land for grazing

Tax due to the lord of the manor

Ashwell, Hertfordshire

Westminster Abbey holds ASHWELL. It answers for 6 hides ... A priest with 16 villagers and 9 smallholders have 5 ploughs; another 5 ploughs possible. 14 burgesses; 9 cottagers. From tolls and other customary dues of the Borough, 49s 4d. 4 slaves. 2 mills at 14s; meadow for 6 ploughs; pasture for the livestock; woodland, 100 pigs. The total value is and was £20; before 1066 £22. Peter the Sheriff holds ½ hide of this land from the Abbot ...

It was Peter de Valognes' duty, as sheriff, to ensure that the king received all that was due to him in the way of revenue and services from Ashwell borough. Later, the Guild of St John, composed of merchants and craftsmen, was involved in running Ashwell. Their Hall still stands in the High Street.

Medieval prosperity was due mainly to the ancient Icknield Way, a trading route that linked Salisbury Plain with the Wash, and the Roman Ashwell Street. But nearby towns

ALFRISTON: *Ship's dragon figurehead outside the Star Inn.*

Alfriston Sussex: *Gilbert and Ranulf from Count of Mortain.* ⌗ Once a medieval market-town; timber-framed buildings; Saxon cemetery by South Downs Way.

ADEL: *A monster swallowing a man's head; rare bronze knocker on the door of St John the Baptist.*

Abbots Morton Worcestershire: *Ranulf from Evesham Church.* ⌗ Black and white timbered houses; once a refuge from outlaw raiders from Feckenham Forest.

Affpuddle Dorset: *Cerne Abbey. 2 mills. 9 oxen.* ⌗ The arms in the church, of the Lawrence family, ancestors of George Washington, are thought to have inspired the United States flag.

Abbotsbury Dorset: *Abbotsbury Abbey; Wife of Hugh FitzGrip. 2 mills. 600 sheep, 23 cattle, 4 cows.* ⌗ Stone-built; famous swannery; tithe barn; remains of an 11th-century Benedictine abbey.

Adel West Riding, Yorkshire: *Count of Mortain and Richard from him.* ⌗ On the outskirts of Leeds; Roman camp; medieval village site.

with navigable rivers and main roads grew while Ashwell languished. Nevertheless, brewing, with agriculture, remained long after the market (first mentioned in 1211) and annual fair (abolished in 1872) had gone.

A magnificent monument to Ashwell's medieval prosperity is its 176ft church tower, begun early in the fourteenth century and built of clunch, a local material midway between chalk and stone.

But soon the Black Death decimated the population; one witness in 1361 recorded his feelings in Latin graffiti inside the tower: 'Miserable, wild and distracted, the dregs of the people alone survive . . .' The entire manor was sold during the Civil War for £416.9.2, but later returned to the See of London.

Today country roads arrive from all directions to tangle in a picturesque knot of streets and lanes. With its wealth of timber-framed buildings, many with overhangs and plaster pargeting, its old inns and old-fashioned shops, Ashwell, especially in and around the church, is strongly rooted in its past.

Ansley Warwickshire: *Nicholas from Countess Godiva.* 🎦 The family of Captain Mark Phillips, husband of Princess Anne, originally came from this mining district.

Algarkirk Lincolnshire: *Colegrim from Abbot of Croyland; Count Alan.* ⚓ Woad mill operated until 1930.

ASHWELL: *The mellow oak of a timbered lime-washed house in its natural colours.*

Bidford on Avon, Warwickshire

[The King holds] BIDFORD (ON AVON). King Edward held it ...; 8 male and 5 female slaves; 28 villagers and 13 smallholders with 16 ploughs. 4 mills at 43s 4d; meadow, 150 acres; woodland 4 leagues long and 1 league wide.

Burstwick East Riding, Yorkshire: *Drogo de Beuvriere.* North Park and South Park show where the Earl of Aumale had his game parks in the mid-13th century.

Bradford Abbas Dorset: *Monks of Sherborne. Mill.* Ancient, stone-built. King Alfred gave the land to Sherborne Abbey in AD 933. Nearby Wyke Farm, a moated manor house, belonged to the monks of Sherborne until the Dissolution.

Benson (Bensington) Oxfordshire: *William from the king; Theodoric the Goldsmith from the king. 2 mills, fisheries.* The lock on the River Thames is where Romans crossed the ford and where Offa of Mercia won a victory over the Saxons in 777.

King Edward held Bidford, thus making it 'ancient demesne', this gave certain privileges, including protection from any attempt by a new lord to exact increased services. So *Domesday* served Bidford well in 1567, in court; the manor was still entitled to freedom from toll throughout the kingdom; exemption from jury service, and from contributing to the expenses of knights of the shire. The town was governed in the seventeenth century by the bailiffs, one of whom signed himself 'His Maieste's Bailiffe of the Burrow of Bidford'. A gilt-brass bailiff's mace with the Tudor royal arms is in the church.

Bidford's history became distinctly secular from the moment the land-grasping and worldly Odo of Bayeux took over. The church went down to final defeat at the Dissolution, when the abbot was refused permission to go on living in Bidford Grange.

The town, nicknamed 'Drunken Bidford', was infamous in the nineteenth century for the drinking bouts of German huntsmen at the Falcon Inn, but the tag is much older, perhaps from the days when William Shakespeare is said to have been a Falcon habitué. At the poet's Birthplace Museum in Stratford-upon-Avon they have both the Inn's furniture and its old sign.

Domesday records four mills at Bidford. One was carried off in the great Avon flood of 1588, but a later paper mill remained until the nineteenth century. Nearby on the River Arrow the corn mill at Great Alne is working again, a pleasant link with the past.

Bridport Dorset: *Bishop of Salisbury; St Wandrille's Abbey.* Town; rope and net-making centre for 1000 years. Parliamentary soldiers almost captured Charles II here in 1651.

Barnbrough West Riding, Yorkshire: *Roger de Bully; William de Warenne. Mill.* The hall was the seat of the Cresacres, one of whom was said to have been killed by a wild cat in the church porch.

Beverley East Riding, Yorkshire: *Archbishop of York and St John's church, Beverley, from him. 3 mills, fishery (7000 eels).* Town. Prosperous mid-12th-century trading centre for wool and cloth. An encompassing 13th-century defensive ditch determined the street pattern.

Bramham West Riding, Yorkshire: *Count of Mortain and Nigel Fossard from him. Mill, church.* Large, recently expanded; church, part Norman, part 13th century; Georgian Bramham Park and gardens.

Boxford Berkshire: *Berner from Abingdon Abbey; Humphrey Visdeloup and Aelfric and Aelmer from him. Mill, church.* On the River Lambourn; mill. Roman coins were found nearby.

BOXFORD: *A peaceful scene on the River Lambourn.*

Bosbury Herefordshire: *Hereford Church. Mill.* Medieval church, the burial-place of the Victorian novelist Edna Lyall.

BOSBURY: *Detached belfry.*

Blyth Nottinghamshire: *Roger de Bully.* In a loop of the River Ryton; 12th-century hospital; 13th-century Angel Inn; Norman arch and north aisle, all that remain of an early priory.

BLYTH: *Mainly Norman church incorporating the remains of the earlier priory.*

The King holds CANTERTON in his Forest. Kenna held it from King Edward, and is still there. Then it paid tax for ½ virgate; now for a quarter; the other quarter lies in the King's Forest. . . . The woodland and meadow lie in the Forest. Value before 1066, 20s; now Kenna, 4s; the King, 16s.

Upper and Lower Canterton lie just outside today's New Forest, with Canterton Manor a few hundred yards to the north. In Canterton Glen the famous Rufus Stone marks the spot where, so the story goes, in the year 1100, William the Conqueror's son, William Rufus, was killed by an arrow while hunting. There have been many explanations of his death: that the Norman Sir Walter Tyrrell shot him by mistake; that William Rufus offered himself as a sacrifice in an ancient fertility rite; and that his brother Henry arranged to have him killed because Henry wanted to marry Eadgyth, daughter of the king of Scotland. Two facts are certain: the church refused Christian burial to the old king; and Henry wasted no time in making himself the next king.

Based on John Leland's 16th-century report that local tradition named the place Thorougham, this was identified as Fritham, just west of Canterton. In 1745 the Rufus Stone was erected in Canterton Glen and in 1841 cased in iron, because it was being chipped away by souvenir hunters. Alas for tradition! Park Farm, 10 miles south-west of Canterton, was originally called Thorougham, and now historians favour this as the murder site.

Canterton itself has altered little in the last 900 years. True, the cottages are now 19th century, but the groves of oak which surround them retain the character of the forest's Ancient and Ornamental Woodlands, and deer still emerge at twilight among the oak and birch of Canterton Glen.

CHICHESTER: *A very fine market cross, given to the city in 1501 by the Bishop.*

Chichester Sussex: *Earl Roger. City, church, mill.* Cathedral city. The medieval town was built over the Roman city, part of whose walls survive. The ancient street plan and a few medieval buildings remain.

Croydon Cambridgeshire : *Earl Roger; Aelmer and Fulkwy from Count Alan; Humphrey from Eudo FitzHubert; 2 men-at-arms from Hardwin of Scales; Ansketel and Alfred from Picot of Cambridge.* Croydon Wilds Wood is famous for birds and butterflies.

Cley next the Sea Norfolk: *King's land.* Small town on the coastal salt marshes. Knucklebone House has cornice and panelling made from sheep's vertebrae.

Coleshill Warwickshire: *King's land. Mill.* Market town.

COLESHILL: *Norman font, 1150, carved with the Evangelists and a crucifixion scene.*

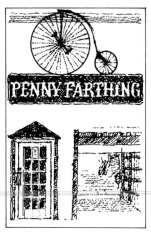

CROWMARSH GIFFORD: *Antique shop with an unusual sign.*

Crowmarsh Gifford Oxfordshire: *Hugh from Walter Giffard, formerly Earl Harold. 2 mills.* Norman church, once a leper hospital.

Cholsey Berkshire: *King's land and Richard Poynant, Gilbert and Hervey from the king, with Abbey of Mont St Michel holding the church. 3 mills.* Partly Norman church.

Caversfield Oxfordshire: *Bryant from William de Warenne. Fishpond.* Caversfield House; Norman church with an early 13th-century bell, the county's oldest.

Cottenham Cambridgeshire: *Abbot of Ely before and after 1066; Crowland Church; Roger from Picot of Cambridge; Picot from Church of Ely and from Church of St Guthlac. 1000 eels.* Many of Samuel Pepys' relatives lived here. A tower windmill is now a water tower.

Cowthorpe West Riding, Yorkshire: *Godefrid from William de Percy. Church.* Secluded; church built in 1450. Cowthorpe Oak was centuries old when John Evelyn's *Sylva* mentioned it (1664).

Chetwynd Shropshire: *Turold from Earl Roger. Mill, 2 fisheries (64 sticks of eels).* Chetwynd mansion and park, haunted by the ghost of Mrs Pigott (one of the family), who died in childbirth.

Childerditch Essex: *Sheriff of Surrey from the king; formerly Queen Edith; Osbern from Swein of Essex, formerly Alwen, a free woman; Sasselin.* Celebrated by Edward Thomas ('If I should ever by chance grow rich/I'll buy Codham, Cockridden and Childerditch').

Constable Burton North Riding, Yorkshire: *Enisan from Count Alan.* Burton Hall, a fine colonnaded house designed by John Carr, is the home of the Wyvills, whose ancestor fought for the Conqueror.

Caversham Berkshire: *Walter Giffard.* District of Reading (across the River Thames) linked by Caversham Bridge. A duel was fought here between Robert de Montfort and Henry of Essex before Henry II in the 12th century.

Croxden Staffordshire: *Alfwold, the pre-Conquest holder, from the king.* The Abbey, the best-preserved monastic ruin in England, was founded for Cistercian monks by Bertram de Verdun in 1176. King John died near here in 1216, ministered to by the monks of Croxden.

Chaddleworth Berkshire: *Winchester Abbey; Robert d'Oilly.* A farmhouse stands on the site of Poughley Priory, whose lands Cardinal Wolsey gave to the Abbot of Westminster in exchange for what is now St James's Park, London.

Chadlington Oxfordshire: *Reginald the Archer and Siward Hunter from the king.* Chadlington Manor House; prehistoric remains on Chadlington downs; trackway, enclosure, standing stone ('The Hawk Stone') and barrows.

Cardington Bedfordshire: *Hugh de Beauchamp; Hugh from Countess Judith. Mill.* Cottages, owned by the Whitbread brewing family in the 18th century. The ill-fated R101 airship was built here.

CASTLE BYTHAM: *The remains of the Norman castle loom over the village.*

Castle Bytham Lincolnshire: *Abbot of Peterborough; Drogo de Beuvriere; Godfrey de Cambrai; Robert of Stafford. 3 ironworks.* Earthworks of the castle built by Drogo de Beuvriere.

Cherrington Shropshire: *Gerard from Earl Roger.* Scattered. The half-timbered moated manor house, dated 1635, is supposed to be the original 'House that Jack built'.

Cooling Kent: *Adam and Odo from Bishop of Bayeux.* Marsh; setting for Charles Dickens' novel *Great Expectations.* 14th-century Cooling Castle was the home of Sir John Oldcastle, the Lollard leader hanged and burned as a heretic in 1417, on whom Shakespeare is said to have modelled his character Falstaff.

Crawley Hampshire: *Hugh from Bishop of Winchester.* Largely 16th century; the inspiration for Queen's Crawley in Thackeray's *Vanity Fair.*

Childwall Lancashire: *Roger de Poitou.* Part of Liverpool. The Calder Stones are from a prehistoric burial mound.

Cookham Berkshire: *King's land. 2 mills, 2 fisheries, market.* On the River Thames. The Saxon Witenagemot met here. The partly Norman church and the Stanley Spencer Gallery both contain work by the painter, who was born here in 1891.

Cheshunt Hertfordshire: *Count Alan, before and after 1066. Mill.* Town with the Waltham Cross, one of the 'Eleanor' crosses erected by Edward I to mark the places where his wife's body rested on its way to London. Cheshunt Great House was the home of Cardinal Wolsey.

COOKHAM: *The tarry stone, a huge boulder that was used as a boundary mark.*

Cossall Nottinghamshire: *William Peverel; Ralph FitzHubert.* The first coal was dug here 7 centuries ago.

Dedham, Essex

Drax West Riding, Yorkshire: *Ralph Pagnell. Church.* 🏚 Norman church tower; perpendicular clerestory, 13th-century chancel.

DRAX: *Charming carved figure, 15th c, in the Norman church of St Peter and St Paul.*

Roger [de Raismes] holds DEDHAM. . . . Then 7 villagers, now 5; always 24 smallholders. Then 4 slaves, now 3. Then 2 ploughs in lordship, now 3. Then among the men 10 ploughs, now 5. Woodland, 250 pigs; meadow, 40 acres; then 1 mill, now 2. Then 2 cobs, now 10; then 5 cows, now 3; then 40 sheep, now 100; then 25 pigs, now 30. Value always £12.

Architecture of at least four centuries mingles discreetly in Dedham from the sixteenth-century Marlborough Head Inn to the neo-Georgian Great House of 1936. The Tudor church of St Mary the Virgin stands in a quiet yard of close-cropped yew trees and gravestones.

There is an inkling of this future prosperity in *Domesday*'s description of the flock of sheep, more than doubled in twenty years. This was the making of wool towns like Dedham, which was, in its prime, intellectually and industrially vigorous.

There is also a note of a second mill, probably the Shirburn mill on the township's eastern boundary. A mill on the earlier site, at the confluence of Black Brook and the River Stour, still dominates the northern approach. Sir John Fastolf was Lord of Dedham Manor, and the model for Shakespeare's Falstaff. In 1450 the real Sir John, a celebrated soldier, elected to the Order of the Garter for his valour against the French, wrote angrily to his agent, instructing him to begin proceedings against a neighbouring parson who had destroyed his new mill and stolen 24 swans and cygnets.

The mill had been re-built when John Constable, born in nearby East Bergholt in 1776, was a schoolboy in Dedham. The village became the centre of his artistic soul, and the tower of St Mary's church figures in several of his landscapes, even where it shouldn't. He sometimes used artistic licence to move it for a better composition!

His paintings eventually influenced official thinking, and in the 1960s Dedham Vale was designated an 'area of outstanding natural beauty'.

Draynes Cornwall: *Alric and Wulfsi, the pre-Conquest holders, from Count of Mortain.* 🏚 Remote; granite cottages and a farm.

Darley Derbyshire: *King's land formerly King Edward. Church. 2 sesters of honey, £40 of pure silver.* 🏚 Church with a Norman font and Burne Jones window. A world-famous yew tree, allegedly England's oldest (2000 years), is in Darley Dale churchyard.

Dolton Devonshire: *Walter Fitz Wimund from Baldwin the Sheriff. 30 cattle, 25 goats.* 🏚 Church with a font made from a carved Saxon cross.

Deerhurst Gloucestershire: *Westminster Abbey.* 🏚 14th-century priory; church with England's finest surviving Saxon font.

DEDHAM VALE (left): *The River Stour, in 'Constable' country.*

DEERHURST (right): *The square tower of one of England's few Saxon buildings rises in this tiny village.*

Edwinstowe, Nottinghamshire

[Land of the King . . .] In EDWINSTOWE. . . . A church and a priest and 4 smallholders have 1 plough. Woodland pasture ½ league long and ½ wide.

EDWINSTOWE: *The legend of Robin Hood and Sherwood forest is so much a part of local history that individual trees have been named – this is one of the candidates for 'Robin's Larder'.*

The only part of Sherwood Forest which Robin Hood might recognize lies slightly to the north. Here some 450 acres known as the Hay of Birklands are wooded with groves of silver birch and astonishing ancient oaks. This, together with the neighbouring Hay of Billhagh probably made up the woodland pasture which belonged to Edwinstowe in 1086.

Here, till a few years ago, stood a massive oak known as 'Robin Hood's larder', from the branches of which he was supposed to have hung his venison. Spectacular as they are, the oaks of the Hay of Birklands are probably no more than 450 years old.

Robin is said to have married Maid Marion in Edwinstowe church. In 1672 the church spire was 'beaten down by thunder'. Seven years later the parishioners humbly petitioned Charles II for 200 trees out of Birkland and Billhagh because 'the whole Body of the Church is shaken and in a very ruinous condition'. This may explain why the present steeple is an irregular polygon. In a wall of the church is a stone eighteen inches long said to have been the standard measure for a 'forest foot'; 30 of these made a perch.

Today the village of Edwinstowe is on the way to the Sherwood Forest Visitors Centre. Its outskirts have grown dismayingly since large-scale coal mining began here in the 1920s but the heart of the original village still has its old houses and a besieged charm.

East Witton North Riding, Yorkshire: *Count Alan.* Attractive, with old houses; Cistercian Abbey of Jervaulx, founded in 1145 and moved to its present site in 1156, nearby. Monks were famous for their Wensleydale cheese. Sedburgh, the last Abbot, was executed at Tyburn for his unwilling part in the Pilgrimage of Grace (1536).

Exford Somerset: *Roger de Courseulles and Ednoth and William from him; William de Mohun.* Kennels of the Devon and Somerset stag-hounds.

Elveden Suffolk: *Count Eustace; Abbot of St Edmund's before and after 1066; Richard FitzGilbert; Nicholas from William de Warenne. 4 churches, fishery. 410 sheep, 94 goats.* Forest; Roman finds; church with a Norman window. Thetford Hall was transformed by the Maharaja Duleep Singh, in the 1860s, into an oriental extravaganza.

Enville Staffordshire: *Gilbert from William FitzAnsculf.* 2 fragments of Saxon work in the church. Enville Hall has belonged to the Grey family for 500 years; its grounds were designed by the poet William Shenstone in the 18th century.

ENVILLE: *A summerhouse, now a museum for Enville Hall.*

Eyham Derbyshire: *King's land.* 8th-century cross in the churchyard; site of an annual well-dressing ceremony.

EYHAM: *Detail from the Saxon cross, weather-worn but still powerful carvings.*

EAST MERSEA: *The Colne estuary in winter.*

Easthope Shropshire: *Rainald the Sheriff from Earl Roger.* 🏠 On Wenlock Edge; Elizabethan manor house.

EASTHOPE: *Replica of an hour glass in an iron grille, in St Peter's Church.*

East Mersea Essex: *Swein of Essex. Beehive. 3 cobs, 12 cattle, 10 pigs, 100 sheep.* 🐝 On Mersea Island; home of Sabine Baring-Gould, author of *Onward Christian Soldiers*, from 1871 to 1881.

East Ham Essex: *St Peter's Westminster; Robert Gernon. 4 cobs.* Part of Greater London.

English Bicknor Gloucestershire: *William FitzNorman.* 🏠 Remains of a motte and bailey castle.

East Farleigh Kent: *Archbishop of Canterbury's monks. 4 mills, 6 fisheries (1200 eels).* 🏠 Fine medieval bridge, over which General Fairfax marched in 1648 to the Battle of Maidstone.

East Bergholt Suffolk: *King's land, in the charge of Aluric Wanz; Aubrey de Vere from Aluric. Mill.* 🏠 Birthplace of the painter John Constable (1776–1837). His father was a miller who owned 16th-century Flatford Mill, the manor house and Willy Lotts cottage.

Epping Essex: *Canons of Waltham before and after 1066; Osbern from Count Alan; 2 free men from Ranulf, brother of Ilger.* Market town; its name means 'the people on the upland'. The old church lies in rural Epping Upland. Epping Forest was originally called Waltham Forest.

Eton Buckinghamshire: *Walter FitzOthere, formerly Queen Edith. 2 mills, fisheries (1000 eels).* Town. Famous for its public school, founded by Henry VI in 1440.

Elham Kent: *Bishop of Bayeux. Church, 2 mills.* 🏠 Large; houses set round a market square; royal charter granted in 1251. The Duke of Wellington made 17th-century Abbot's Fireside his temporary headquarters during the Napoleonic Wars.

Easingwold North Riding, Yorkshire: *King's land. Church.* Small market town with a bull-ring and old houses. The church is mostly 14th century.

Eaton Bray Bedfordshire: *Bishop of Bayeux.* 🏠 Large, pretty; timber-framed buildings.

EATON BRAY: *Door of the 13th-c. church.*

Framlingham, Suffolk

Aelmer, a thane, held FRAMLINGHAM. Now R(oger) Bigot holds (it) [from Earl Hugh]. Then 24 villagers, now 32; then 16 smallholders, now 28. Then 5 ploughs in lordship, now 3; then 20 men's ploughs, now 16. Woodland, 100 pigs; meadow, 16 acres. Then 2 cobs, now 3; then 4 cattle, now 7; then 40 pigs, now 10; then 20 sheep, now 40; always 60 goats; now 3 beehives. Value then £16; now £36.

In the same (Framlingham) Munulf held, half under the patronage of Aelmer and half under (that) of Malet's predecessor; 1 carucate of land and 40 acres as a manor. Always 4 villagers; 12 smallholders; 2 ploughs in lordship; 2½ men's ploughs. Woodland, 100 pigs; meadow, 6 acres. 8 cattle, 20 pigs, 60 sheep, 40 goats, 4 beehives. Value always 40s. William Malet was in possession. Under him, 6 whole free men and 4 half (free) men; 30 acres of land. Always 1 plough. Meadow, 1 acre. They are in the assessment of 40s. In the same (Framlingham) 1 free man under patronage; 40 acres, 1 villager who dwells in *Ethereg*; 3 smallholders. Meadow, 1 acre. 1 plough. Woodland, 4 pigs. Value 8s. In the same (Framlingham) 3 free men under patronage; 56 acres. Always 3 ploughs. Meadow, 2 acres; woodland, 4 pigs. Value 17s. 1 church, 60 acres. 1 villager; 4 smallholders. 2 ploughs. Value 15s. In length 14 furlongs, and 12 in width; 20d in tax. [St] Etheldreda's (had) the jurisdiction but (Earl) Hugh's predecessor had it from it.

This is a charming little town with neat streets, prosperous houses and sloping market place and far less important than its *Domesday* self must have been. From the outside St Michael's is as tranquil as its surroundings. The chancel tells another story, crowded with the sixteenth-century tombs of the Howards of Norfolk, a mausoleum of vanity and bloodshed.

Nearby is Framlingham Castle, a tall, irregular circle of grey stone. A castle stood here in Saxon times, perhaps as early as the sixth century. King Edmund, it is said, sought protection within its walls from the Danes, but was driven forth and murdered in the forests which covered much of this region.

John Evelyn in his *Discourse of Forest Trees* (1664) praised Framlingham for its magnificent oaks, the finest 'perhaps in the world'. And the seventeenth-century warship *Royal Sovereign*, the flagship of King Charles II's navy, was built of Framlingham oak.

Roger Bigot's manor had grown substantially since the Conquest. His total of 19 ploughs indicates that a large area had been cleared for crops, a sign of a prosperous community. Framlingham suffered less in the transition from Saxon to Norman rule than many neighbouring settlements. But why there were so many goats – well above the local average – is one of the many minor curiosities of *Domesday*.

The Bigot family (especially Roger's son, the scheming and ruthless Hugh) became warlords of Suffolk. Subsequent castle owners continued to fall foul of royalty. The Howards, Dukes of Norfolk, who took possession late in the fifteenth century, had a disastrous history, from the first duke, who backed the losing side in the Battle of Bosworth, to the fifth, beheaded for plotting to free Mary Queen of Scots.

Edward VI held his first court here at Framlingham Castle and his sister Mary proclaimed herself queen while rallying her forces against the armies of Lady Jane Grey. There is a legend that, during her stay, she 'gave birth to a monster, which ... she instantly destroyed' on a stone pointed out to eighteenth-century travellers. By then Framlingham had ceased to have any political or military importance. The inside of the castle was gutted and a workhouse, which still stands, was built within the walls. This picturesque shell and the proud tombs are all that remain of grandeur.

Faversham Kent: *King's land.* 2 salt-houses, mill, market. Market town and small port. Richard Arden, a 16th-century mayor, was murdered here by his wife and her lover. An early domestic drama, *Arden of Faversham*, is based on this story.

Frilsham Berkshire: *Roger from Henry de Ferrers. Mill.* 🖼 The church is dedicated to St Frideswide, a Saxon princess who founded a convent in the forest; Frilsham House.

Faceby North Riding, Yorkshire: *King's land.* 🖼 Roman finds here. Charity loaves are still given away here after a will of 1634.

Frindsbury Kent: *Bishop of Rochester. Church, mill.* 🖼 Church founded in 1075 still stands; cement-works.

Frampton-on-Severn Gloucestershire: *Drogo FitzPoyntz (Roger de Lacy wrongfully holds 1 hide). Mill.* 🖼 On a canal; half-timbered houses; large village green. Frampton Court is a Georgian manor house.

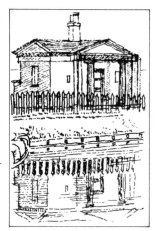

FRAMPTON-ON-SEVERN: *A house on the Sharpness Canal.*

Folkestone Kent: *William de Arques from Bishop of Bayeux.* 5 churches, 11½ mills, salt-house. Seaside resort and fishing port; birthplace of William Harvey, the physician who discovered blood circulation. East Cliff has remains of a Roman villa, but Caesar's Camp is Norman. The 13th-century parish church stands on the site of a 7th-century Saxon nunnery.

Farnham Surrey: *Bishop of Winchester before and after 1066 and Ralph, William and Wace from him.* 6 mills. Town which once had the county's most important corn market. Prehistoric and Roman remains have been discovered here. A castle, built in Norman times, is now partly a conference centre.

Fylingdales North Riding, Yorkshire: *William de Percy.* Mainly barren moorland; site of Fylingdales Early Warning System since 1961–62. Originally Fyling and North Fyling.

FYLINGDALES (overleaf): *One of the principal settlements is Robin Hood's Bay, a picturesque fishing village.*

Grantchester, Cambridgeshire

In GRANTCHESTER Robert [Fafiton] holds 2 hides and 3 virgates. . . . 4 villagers with 7 smallholders have 2 ploughs. 22 cottagers. 1 mill at 40s; from ½ weir 500 eels. In total the value is and was £7; before 1066 £10. 4 Freemen held this land . . . they could grant and sell their lands.

If medieval fables are to be believed, Grantchester was one of Britain's great cities when the Romans arrived. Until the Cam was bridged at Cambridge, Grantchester, with its two fords, lay on a busy east–west route. By the time of *Domesday* its land was in the hands of six nobles, by far the two largest holdings belonging to Count Eustace and Robert Fafiton. Each of these held equal areas of land and each owned a mill. The fishery at nearby Doddington paid 27,150 eels annually. Grantchester's 500 was a peppercorn rent in comparison.

'The whole place is very lovely, with apple blossom now, later with roses. Will you come and stay here?' wrote the poet Rupert Brooke to a friend in 1910. 'I can promise you bathing and all manner of rustic delight.'

Grantchester retains at least a few delights that Brooke would recognize. It is still an easy walk across pleasant fields south from Cambridge. The River Cam still flows neatly between grassy banks and pruned trees. The church clock, however, is something of a disappointment. Immortalized by Brooke, in his poem 'The Old Vicarage Grantchester', as stopped perpetually at ten to three, it has kept excellent time for many years.

An ordinance of 1802 forbade the owners of hogs to let their animals roam the street, but in spite of such attempts at modernization, it was not until 1834 that the main road to Cambridge was suitable for wheeled vehicles.

The weir and both the mills are thought to have been where Byron's Pool is today. (The young Lord Byron had discovered the delights of Grantchester a century before Brooke, when he was an undergraduate at Cambridge.)

'It does not appear that there have been any celebrated persons who have lived or been born here,' lamented a nineteenth-century local historian. That was before the doomed and handsome Rupert Brooke moved to Grantchester in 1909. Brooke's nostalgic celebration of his adopted home has made the village a symbol of a lost, innocent England.

Gloucester Gloucestershire: *King's land; Gloucester Abbey both before and after 1066. 5 fisheries, mill.* Cathedral city, formerly Roman; 18th-century and older houses. The 'New' Inn is a 15th-century Pilgrims' Hostel. William I commissioned the *Domesday* survey here at his Christmas council in 1085.

Great Addington Northamptonshire: *Hugh from Bishop of Coutances; Peterborough Abbey. 3 mills (200 eels).* 🏚 Scene of 17th-century riot between peasants and gentry; Roman graves on nearby Shooters Hill.

Great Smeaton North Riding, Yorkshire: *King's land; Count Alan.* 🏚 Manor; church is the only one in England to be dedicated to St Eloy, the blacksmith's saint.

Grimley Worcestershire: *Worcester Church. Mill, ½ fishery (sticks of eels).* 🏚 Napoleon's brother, Lucien, lived here after he was captured by the British in 1810.

GRANTCHESTER: *View towards Cambridge from the banks of the River Cam.*

GREAT CHESTERFORD: *An ancient timbered cottage.*

Great Chesterford Essex: *Picot the Sheriff in the king's hand. 2 mills.* ▨ Remains of Belgic settlement; Roman fort and town.

Gilling East North Riding, Yorkshire: *Ralph de Mortimer; Hugh FitzBaldric.* ▨ Gilling Castle, a 14th–18th-century house, is now a prep school for Ampleforth College.

Gittisham Devon: *Gotshelm. Mill. 2 cobs.* ▨ Bronze Age barrows. The Rolling Stone, said to be the site of human sacrifices, is nearby; when the moon is full, it rolls down to the River Sid to cleanse itself of blood.

Godmersham Kent: *Archbishop of Canterbury. Church, mill.* ▨ On River Stow. Jane Austen visited her brother at Godmersham Park and based her novel *Mansfield Park* there.

Goodmanham East Riding, Yorkshire: *King's land; Archbishop of York; Nigel Fossard from Count of Mortain; William de Colevil from William de Percy; Gilbert de Tison.* ▨ Tumuli; Norman church built over a pagan temple destroyed in 627 after King Edwin had been converted.

Gop Wales: *Robert of Rhuddlan.* Gop Hill; cairn, possibly Bronze Age; caves, in use *c.*4000–2000 BC, in which the bones of humans and the woolly rhino were found.

Great Coxwell Berkshire: *King's land. Church.* ▨ Great Barn, shaped like a cross and built by the monks of Beaulieu in the 13th century, has been restored and is in use.

Great Torrington Devon: *Roger from Ralph de Pomeroy; Ansger de Montacute; Odo FitzGamelin and 3 Frenchmen from him. 12 cattle, 146 sheep.* Town and market centre since Saxon times, with a park on the site of a Norman castle. The church was blown up in 1645 with 200 Royalists inside.

Greenwich Kent: *Bishop of Lisieux from Bishop of Bayeux.* Thames-side London borough; developed by the Stuart kings. The royal palace was the birthplace of Henry VIII, Queen Mary and Elizabeth I.

Grinshill Shropshire: *Walchelin from Earl Roger.* ▨ Pretty; source of the 'white' stone used by the Romans to build *Viriconium*; Stone Grange, built or bought by Shrewsbury School as a refuge from the plague *c.*1617.

Great Easton Leicestershire: *Peterborough Abbey.* ▨ Large; Romano-British remains.

Groton Suffolk: *King's land, kept by William the Chamberlain and Otto the Goldsmith; Abbot of St Edmund's before and after 1066; Richard FitzGilbert.* ▨ Home of John Winthrop, who organized local migration to America and became governor of Massachusetts, 1660–76. A church window, in his memory, was donated by New England Winthrops.

Godalming Surrey: *King's land with Ranulf Ilambard holding 2 churches. 3 mills.* Town, well known for its inns in coaching times. One of its churches has 2 blocked Saxon windows.

GODALMING: *The delightful and tiny town hall houses a museum of local antiquities; the site has been in use for over 1000 years.*

[Earl Hugh holds] HAWARDEN in lordship. Earl Edwin held it . . . Land for 4½ ploughs. 4 slaves; a church . . . 4 villagers and 6 smallholders . . . Meadow . . . woodland 2 leagues long and 1 wide. Value 40s. 2 unoccupied dwellings in the City belong to there.

Once in Cheshire, the nineteenth-century Hawarden Castle was the home of William Ewart Gladstone. A wave from 'the greatest Englishman of the century' would send hundreds of tourists home exhilarated by their pilgrimage. This was one of the few moments of fame for a low, dark village.

Domesday mentions a church, St Deiniol's, one of only nine recorded for the entire county of Cheshire. It was here, according to legend, that a figure of the Virgin Mary fell from the roodloft and killed the wife of the castle's governor. The statue was put to trial by jury and condemned to death by drowning, but it floated up the River Dee and was washed ashore at Chester in 946.

The region's inaccessibility may have preserved it from the wrath of King William, who had laid waste much of the rest of the county in 1070. The number of working ploughs in Hawarden – four, where there was land for four and a half – also suggests that the village had not suffered too badly.

There was still plenty of woodland in the nineteenth century and Mr Gladstone took great pleasure in chopping down trees. He was felling a tree in 1868 when the telegram arrived asking him to be Prime Minister. 'My mission is to pacify Ireland,' he optimistically announced, and continued to chop until the tree had fallen.

HEMEL HEMPSTEAD: *Formerly a street pump, dated 1848.*

HAYES: *The Tapsel gate at St Mary's church.*

Hayes Middlesex: *Archbishop Lanfranc. Mill.* Town engulfed by modern housing.

Halliggye Cornwall: *King's land, part of Winnianton Manor; Thurstan.* Halliggye Fougou, an underground chamber with a long main passage similar to those found near Iron Age settlements.

Halkyn Cheshire: *Earl Hugh; Robert of Rhuddlan. Church; mill.* 19th-century Halkyn Castle. Halkyn Mountain has been a lead-mining area since Roman times.

Havant Hampshire: *Bishop of Winchester. 2 mills, 3 salt-houses.* Town. Parchment has been made here for nearly 1000 years.

Harewood West Riding, Yorkshire: *King's land.* Ruins of a 12th-century castle. 18th-century Harewood House has grounds by Capability Brown.

Hampole West Riding, Yorkshire: *Roger de Bully. ½ mill.* Castle mound. Richard Rolle (d.1349), the mystical writer, lived as a hermit here and is buried in the church of the now vanished Cistercian nunnery.

Helston Cornwall: *King's land, formerly Earl Harold. 14 unbroken mares, 200 sheep, 40 ale-men, who probably paid their dues in beer.* Market town, celebrated for its annual Furry (Floral) dance.

Heptonstall West Riding, Yorkshire: *King's land, formerly King Edward. 2 churches.* Old hand-weaving centre; steep streets; weavers' cottages.

Hessle West Riding, Yorkshire: *Malger from Ilbert de Lacy; 6 iron workers.* Remains of bell-pits, used for ironstone extraction. This is one of *Domesday's* few allusions to Yorkshire iron making. The monasteries later took up the industry.

Hidcote Bartrim Gloucestershire: *2 men-at-arms from Evesham Abbey.* Hidcote Manor's gardens were created by Lawrence Johnston in 1905.

Hinton Waldrist Berkshire: *Odo, the king's thane, formerly Wulfwen, a woman. Church, 2 fisheries.* Elizabethan Hinton Manor, with moat; near a Roman earthwork, known as Hadchester or Adchester.

Hitcham Suffolk: *Abbot of Ely and Roger Bigot from him; Richard FitzGilbert and Ailward son of Bell from him. Church.* Romano-British settlement site nearby. John Henslow, who influenced Darwin and secured his appointment to the *Beagle,* was rector here from 1837.

Hathersage Derbyshire: *Ralph FitzHubert.* According to tradition, the grave of Little John, Robin Hood's follower, is in the churchyard.

Houghton Huntingdonshire: *Ramsey Abbey. Church, mill.* Attractive; 17th-century watermill on the site of a mill given by the 10th-century founder of Ramsey Abbey to the abbot.

Hemel Hempstead Hertfordshire: *Count of Mortain. 4 mills. 300 eels.* Market town, one of the first New Towns; Norman church with Roman bricks.

Huntshaw Devonshire: *William Cheever. 10 cattle, 100 sheep, 30 goats.* Mainly 15th-century church with a 12th-century chancel; all who helped rebuild it in 1439 were granted indulgences.

HOUGHTON: *Tenants of Ramsey Abbey were heavily fined if they did not use the abbey mill on this site.*

Heysham Lancashire: *King's land.* Coastal town close to Morecambe, with a nuclear power station and ferry port. St Patrick is said to have come ashore here when he was shipwrecked in Morecambe Bay.

Hinxworth Hertfordshire: *2 men-at-arms from William d'Eu; Peter de Valognes; Theobald from Hardwin of Scales.* The 15th-century historian Robert Clutterbuck lived at Hinxworth Place. A Roman Venus was found here, and a pre-Roman gravel pit revealed traces of 4 British tribes.

Hawksworth Nottinghamshire: *Walter d'Aincourt; Gilbert de Ghent.* Fenland; site of a Wars of the Roses battlefield.

Huntingfield Suffolk: *Walter FitzAubrey from Robert Malet's mother. Church. 6 beehives.* Once part of the estate given to Anne of Cleves by Henry VIII; church with Norman work.

Hornby Lancashire: *Orm and Ulf from the king.* Rebuilt but romantic-looking castle described by Scott in *Marmion;* Castle Stede, a Norman earthwork, nearby.

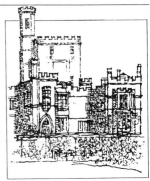

HEYSHAM: *Near St Patrick's Church is a strange graveyard hewn out of the rock.*

HORNBY: *The Castle was demolished in 1643, and its walls rebuilt later.*

Ingarsby, Leicestershire

[Ivo] also holds 12 c. of land in INGARSBY from Hugh [de Grandmesnil]. Land for 8 ploughs. In lordship 2; 4 male and 1 female slaves. 16 villagers with 7 smallholders and 1 man-at-arms with 3 Frenchmen have 5 ploughs. A mill at 4s. The value was 40s; now £4.

Ingarsby is now only a series of mounds and depressions spreading over two sloping meadows in the countryside near Hungerton, a few miles east of Leicester. But *Domesday* shows that in 1086 it was a larger than average settlement.

The village was granted to Leicester Abbey in 1352, except for a few bits which it bought up over the next hundred years. There were five major outbreaks of bubonic plague in Leicestershire between 1349 and 1400, depleting the population by up to a half and bringing about an agricultural depression. As a result, the abbey enclosed the estate with hedges and ditches in 1469 and converted it into a sheep and cattle ranch. This appears to have caused the desertion of the village, says a plaque on the site.

Ingarsby was one of perhaps 1000 villages which were cleared for sheep between 1450 and 1600. 'Thirty persons departed in tears and have perished', wrote a contemporary of the clearance of nearby Willowes in 1495. Dispossessed peasants wandered the roads, robbing travellers or poaching to stay alive, while Parliament passed a series of Acts in a vain attempt to halt the 'Pulling Down of Towns'. The peasant uprisings of 1607 in Leicestershire, Northamptonshire and Warwickshire were a direct reaction to these clearances. Protesting 'diggers' cut down hedges and filled in ditches used to enclose old arable land, while sympathizers supplied them with spades and food. They warned anyone against trying to stop them by force: '… better it were in such a case we manfully die than hereafter to be pined to death for want of that which these devouring encroachers do serve their fat hogs and sheep withal … They have depopulated and overthrown whole towns and made thereof sheep pastures, nothing profitable for our commonwealth.'

Civil order was restored without too much trouble, and today Ingarsby and much of the land around it is still pasture. From low on the opposite slopes, it is easy to see the irregular rectangular pattern of banks and shallow ditches where ancient houses once stood. The pond at the bottom, now overgrown by trees, was probably dug by the abbey as a fishpond. Large earth ramparts enclose the whole area, which villagers would have patrolled, keeping a night watch against marauders.

INGESTRE: *The Royal Arms in the church; dated 1676.*

Ingestre Staffordshire: *Hugh from Robert of Stafford. Part of a mill.* ⚓ Hall with a Wren-built church, and a Nash front, where Edward VII spent his holidays, damaged by fire in 1882.

Iwerne Courtney (or Shroton) Dorset: *Baldwin the Sheriff. 2 mills.* 🏰 At the foot of 600ft Hambledon Hill (with its Iron Age fort), where General Wolfe trained his troops before scaling the Heights of Abraham to attack Quebec in 1759.

Impington Cambridgeshire: *Abbot of Ely before and after 1066; Walter from Picot of Cambridge.* ⚓ Home of Samuel Pepys. The Village College, designed by Walter Gropius and Maxwell Fry, was opened in 1938.

Jevington Sussex: *Hugh from Count of Eu, Ralph from Count of Mortain. Mill.* 🏰 Neolithic causeway camp on Combe Hill; Bronze Age barrow nearby; church with a Saxon tower.

INGARSBY (overleaf): *The shadows which show so much about our lost villages are most revealing in the early morning or late afternoon and evening.*

IDE: *A thatched cottage with unusual windows.*

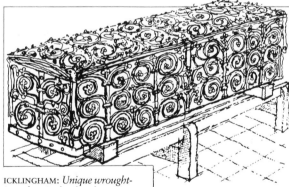

ICKLINGHAM: *Unique wrought-iron chest in the church.*

Icklingham Suffolk: *King's land, kept by William de Noyers; Ranulph Peverel; Moruant from Eudo FitzSpirwic. Church, 2 mills.* 🏰 2 parish churches; site of a Roman villa.

Isle Farm Shropshire: *Rainald the Sheriff from Earl Roger. Mill.* 17th-century Isle House; remains of medieval fishponds. The loop of the River Severn nearly forms an island.

Ingleby Derbyshire: *King's land. Ralph FitzHubert and Nigel of Stafford, the pre-Conquest holders from the king. Mill site.* ⚓ Pagan cemetery (AD 800–950) with over 50 burial mounds, in Heath Wood.

Idleberg Gloucestershire: *Evesham Abbey: Lost.* The Four Shire Stone, marking the meeting-place of Gloucestershire, Warwickshire and Oxfordshire, is all that remains.

Ilfracombe Devonshire: *Robert from Baldwin the Sheriff. Cob, 133 sheep.* Seaside resort with an important harbour since the 13th century, when St Nicholas's Chapel on Lantern Hill was the cell of a hermit who kept a light to guide shipping.

Ide Devonshire: *Bishop of Exeter. Cob.* 🏰 13th-century bridge; group of 17th-century cottages called 'The College'.

King's Cliffe, Northamptonshire

The King holds (KING'S) CLIFFE. Earl Algar held it. Land for 14 ploughs ... 7 villagers with a priest and 6 smallholders who have 5 ploughs. A mill at 12d; meadow, 4 acres; woodland 1 league long and ½ league wide. It paid £7 before 1066; now £10.

King William made King's Cliffe a royal manor and so it remained until early in the nineteenth century, often part of a marriage settlement for a new queen of England.

The comparatively small amount of cultivated land contrasts tellingly with the large tract of woodland – over a square mile. The first reference to a hunting lodge, the King's House, was in Henry II's time.

By early in the fourteenth century the royal seat of 'Clive', as it was called, was one of the district's most flourishing towns. It had a market and a three-day fair where a popular article was excellent turned wood. During the fairs, placing a bough of wood on the doorstep of a private home instantly transformed it into a licensed ale-house!

A central tower had been added to the church around 1100 and later a handsome broach spire, a sure sign of prosperity. Two mills were grinding corn in 1650, one of which still survives.

One of the worst of a number of fires occurred in 1462 when 100 houses were destroyed, including the Manor House where Kings Edward I and II had stayed. A document of about 1439 reveals that numerous houses were 'waste' – returning no revenue to the king. The town's decline was severe enough for the authorities to suspend the market and fair. These were not reinstated until 1604.

Michael Hudson, Rector of King's Cliffe during the Civil War, undertook dangerous courier work for the king, and was captured three times by Cromwell's men. He was released once and escaped twice, the second time in disguise with a basket of apples on his head. In 1648 at Woodcroft Castle, Parliamentarian troops stormed the stronghold and forced Hudson over the battlements into the moat beneath. After he was dead, his tongue was cut out and carried about as a trophy.

King's Cliffe today is no more than a large village. Its population is now slowly expanding, but it has never truly recovered from its late medieval decline.

KIRBY: *The ruins of Kirby Hall from the south.*

Kirby Northamptonshire: *Richard.* Ruins of hall begun in 1570 and added to by Inigo Jones.

Knowlton Kent: *Thurstan from Bishop of Bayeux.*

Kewstoke Somerset: *Osbern from Gilbert FitzThorold. 5 unbroken mares, 18 cattle.* Adjoining Weston-super-Mare. The Becket Cup in Taunton Museum is purportedly a relic containing the blood of Thomas à Becket.

Kimbolton Huntingdonshire: *William de Warenne, formerly Earl Harold. Church, mill.* 13th–14th century church. Katherine of Aragon spent her last unhappy years in virtual confinement in Kimbolton Castle.

KIMBOLTON (right): *The church dates from the 13th and 14th c. and almost certainly stands on the site of the* Domesday *church.*

KING'S CLIFFE (left): *Warm honey-coloured stone is used for almost all the village houses.*

Lyme Regis, Dorset

LITTLE GIDDING: The tiny 17th-c. church has been restored, and contains a unique brass font.

[The Bishop of Salisbury holds] LYME (REGIS) . . . It has never paid tax. Fishermen hold it; they pay 15s to the monks [of Sherborne] for fish . . . The Bishop has 1 house there which pays 6d.

———

The Church [of St Mary's, Glastonbury] holds LYME (REGIS) itself . . . Wulfgeat held and holds it from the Abbot. He has 2 ploughs and 9 villagers and 6 smallholders and meadow . . . pasture . . . woodland . . . 13 saltworkers who pay 13s. Value of the whole 60s.

———

William Bellett also holds LYME (REGIS). Aelfeva held it before 1066 . . . 1 villager with ½ plough; 14 salt-workers. A mill which pays 39d; meadow . . . pasture . . . woodland . . . Value 60s.

Three separate manors formed this curious little fishing port clustered at the foot of the cliffs so steep that there was no descent for wheeled vehicles until 1759. The town is mentioned as far back as the eighth century; its curved stone jetty, The Cobb, is believed to have stood for more than one thousand years and must surely have been

used by the fishermen mentioned in *Domesday*. It achieved a measure of immortality when Jane Austen set Louisa Musgrove's dramatic accident there in *Persuasion* and John Fowles used it as a feature in *The French Lieutenant's Woman*.

The town played a part in the many battles of the seventeenth century. Prince Maurice marched here with his army in 1644 against the Parliamentary forces in the town. The siege failed, partly because supplies arrived by sea, and partly because of the town's women. Dressed as soldiers to confuse the enemy, they fought valiantly beside their men.

In 1685 the foolish and ill-starred protestant Duke of Monmouth, natural son of Charles II, landed west of The Cobb, to begin his hopeless attempt to usurp the English throne from his Catholic uncle James II. He picked this particular beach because The Cobb was guarded by a fort with five cannon which he hoped to capture. That there was no powder for them, he was not to know.

With townsmen cheering him on, Monmouth marched up to the market-place. His notorious Declaration there cost him his life little more than a month later. Among other fantasies it accused King James of having started the Great Fire of London and of poisoning Charles II to secure the Crown. But the townsfolk, openly anti-Catholic, were smitten by the handsome Duke. Marching north from Lyme Regis, he amassed more than 2000 followers, all badly armed and without military discipline.

At Sedgemoor, the king's forces crushed Monmouth's men. Two days later 'The little Duke' was captured hiding in a ditch. A week later, he was beheaded at the Tower.

And there was more blood to be spilled. The sadistic Judge Jeffreys extracted a high price for the West Country's folly; that September alone 800 men were transported and 300 hanged. It was a nightmare landscape after the Lord Chief Justice had passed, with human heads and dismembered bodies adorning all the highways and cross-roads. Twelve men were hanged at the Duke's landing-place.

With tourism its major industry Lyme has lost a lot of its personality in self-conscious attempts to preserve it. But still the little fishing boats leave from The Cobb in pursuit of mackerel, prawns and conger-eel, keeping alive a way of life that *Domesday* recorded 900 years ago.

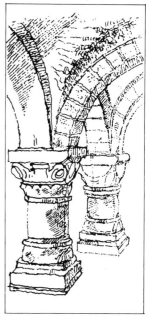

LASTINGHAM: *The Norman crypt (1075–85) has low heavy columns.*

Lastingham North Riding, Yorkshire: *King's land; Abbot of York from Berengar de Tosny.* Roman and Saxon remains found here; late Norman church incorporates part of an 11th-century abbey.

Lacock Wiltshire: *Edward of Salisbury; Alfred of Marlborough. 2 mills, vineyard.* One of England's most beautiful abbeys, founded as an Augustinian nunnery, 1229. W.H. Fox Talbot, father of photography, carried out his experiments here, in 1839.

Littleton Pannell Wiltshire: *William d'Audrieu from William d'Eu.* à Becket 's house; 18th-century manor house.

Linby Nottinghamshire: *William Peverel. Mill.* Mining; stream and converted Castle Mill with water wheel. Stone crosses nearby are thought to mark the ancient boundaries of Sherwood Forest.

Liddington Wiltshire: *Abbess of Shaftesbury. 2 mills.* Iron Age earthworks, Liddington Castle; Elizabethan manor house.

Laver Essex: *Count Eustace and Richard from him; Roger from Ralph de Tosny.* Now 3 hamlets, High, Little and Magdalen Laver. John Locke the publisher had a library of 4000 books at High Laver in the late 17th century; Roman remains were found at Little Laver.

Longner Shropshire: *Bishop of Chester and Wigot from him.* Hall by John Nash. Edward Burton, a Protestant zealot, who died from joy on learning that Elizabeth I had acceded to the throne, is buried in its garden.

Lockeridge Wiltshire: *Durand of Gloucester.* On the River Kennet, Lockeridge House, Georgian.

Leckhampton Gloucestershire: *William Leofric; Britric from the king.* Adjacent to Cheltenham. Stone for Regency Cheltenham came from the precipitous cliff called Devil's Chimney.

Lancaster Lancashire: *King's land.* County town and city on the River Lune, once a large port, named after a Roman camp, and dominated by its castle with a Norman keep. The priory church of St Mary's, on a Roman site, has Anglo-Saxon work and 14th-century choirstalls.

LANCASTER: *Williamson's Park, setting for a folly built by Lord Ashton.*

Little Barningham Norfolk: *King's land, in the custody of Godric; William de Warenne; Bishop William; Brant from Robert FitzCorbucion. Church, mill.* A church pew, made by Stephen Crosbie in 1640, with a carved skeleton and the inscription: 'As you are now, ever so was I', is reserved for 'couples joined in wedlock'.

Leyburn North Riding, Yorkshire: *Wihomarc from Count Alan.* Small market town; tradition has it that Mary Queen of Scots was captured on the limestone terrace, Leyburn Shawl, after escaping from Bolton Castle.

Lytchett Matravers Dorset: *William d'Eu.* Ancient. Becoming a suburb of Bournemouth and Poole. Sir John Matravers, buried in the 13th-century church, was Edward III's gaoler and probable murderer.

Letchworth Hertfordshire: *William from Robert Gernon.* Garden city (founded 1903 by Ebenezer Howard as a pioneering example of urban planning). The central highway is the prehistoric Icknield Way.

Littlehempston Devonshire: *King's land, formerly Earl Harold. Ralph de Pomeroy from Iudhael of Totnes. 40 goats.* Old Manor, c.1400 with a 15th-century fresco.

Ludgvan Cornwall: *Richard from Count of Mortain. 27 unbroken mares.* Nearby is Chysauster, England's oldest village street, c.100 BC to 3rd century AD.

Laverstoke Hampshire: *St Peter's, Winchester, formerly Wulfeva Beteslau, a woman who held it until her death when the king returned it to the church for the sake of his soul and that of his wife.* Laverstoke House and park. Paper for bank notes has been made here since the 18th century.

Launceston Cornwall: *Count of Mortain. 2 mills, castle. 5 cattle, 50 sheep.* Cornwall's only walled town, with the ruins of the castle mentioned in *Domesday.*

LAUNCESTON: *The ruins of the castle mentioned in* Domesday; *a circular tower and the shell of the keep remain.*

Much Wenlock, Shropshire

The Church [of St Milburga] itself holds (Much) WENLOCK, it held it before 1066. 20 hides; 4 of them were exempt from tax in King Canute's time, the others paid tax. ... 9 villagers, 3 riders and 46 smallholders; between them they have 17 ploughs; another 17 would be possible there. 15 slaves. 2 mills which serve the monks. 1 fishery; woodland for fattening 300 pigs; 2 hedged enclosures. Value before 1066 £15; now £12.

Inside the old borough town, like a cocoon in a wall cranny, lies concealed possibly the finest medieval domestic house in Britain – once the infirmary and prior's house of the Cluniac abbey. The foundation had been started by St Milburga, the granddaughter of Penda, King of Mercia.

In 1322 Walter de Caldebrook paid six shillings to the abbey to 'dig for seacoal in Le Brocholes' (still identifiable between Ironbridge and Madeley). St Milburga's had its own coal mines at Little Wenlock and at Broseley; and its own iron foundries in Shirlett Forest. Today the churchyard at Little Wenlock has not only iron tombstones but iron urns and plinths as well.

After 1709, Abraham Darby's concentration of a previously dispersed iron industry – coke furnace, forge and engineering works close together and connected by railway – brought about the astounding growth of the steel industry early in the nineteenth century. It is no exaggeration to say that the forge hammer which was to be heard around the world first began to strike on iron smelted with coke amidst the woodlands of the ancient lands of St Milburga.

But still Much Wenlock is probably better known for its Olympic Games, founded by Dr William Penny Brook, which helped to trigger the revival in 1896 of the international Olympic Games.

MORETON CORBET: *House incorporating castle ruins.*

Moreton Corbet Shropshire: *Turold from Earl Roger.* Ruins of an Elizabethan house, incorporating parts of an earlier castle.

Moreton Say Shropshire: *Roger de Lacy from Earl Roger.* Clive of India (1725–74) was born at nearby Styche Hall.

Morville Shropshire: *Earl Roger with Church of St Peter, Shrewsbury holding the church and Richard the Butler and the earl's chaplains from Earl Roger. Mill.* Elizabethan Morville Hall; church with many Norman features including a font and door ironwork.

Myddle Shropshire: *Rainald the Sheriff from Earl Roger.* Circular stair turret of castle. Richard Gough's *History of Myddle* is a graphic chronicle of the village in the 17th century.

Maiden Bradley Wiltshire: *Walter Giffard from the king. 2 mills.* Priory Farm on the site of a 12th-century leper hospital, later an Augustinian priory.

Matlock Derbyshire: *King's land.* Spa and beauty spot known as 'Little Switzerland', written of by Byron and D. H. Lawrence; caverns and spring at High Tor.

Much Hadham Hertfordshire: *Bishop of London and William and Osbern from him; Abbot of Ely. Mill.* Hadham Palace, now a farmhouse, was the country home of the bishops of London for 800 years. Henry V's widow Catherine gave birth here to Edmund Tudor, father of Henry VI.

MUCH WENLOCK: *The priory was a Cluniac abbey from the 10th c. until the Dissolution.*

MORETONHAMPSTEAD: *The almshouses with arcades.*

Moretonhampstead

Devonshire: *Baldwin from the king, formerly Earl Harold. 20 cattle, 130 sheep.* Small market town on Dartmoor with 17th-century almshouses, old wayside crosses nearby include Horspit Cross. The church has tombstones of Napoleonic prisoners of war.

Mavesyn Ridware

Staffordshire: *Ascelin from Earl Roger.* 🐎 Named after the Mavesyn family, called Mal-voisins (bad neighbours) in Norman times.

March Cambridgeshire: *Abbot of Ely; St Edmund's.* A market town with large railway marshalling yard, it was a hamlet until the 19th century and the coming of the railway.

MARCH: *120 angels, 12 Apostles and the devil are carved on this magnificent medieval church roof.*

Marston St Lawrence

Northamptonshire: *Earl Hugh. Mill.* 🏠 Manor house. Charles Chauncy, 17th-century vicar, became President of Harvard University in the US.

MONTACUTE: *Gable of the house built by Ed. Phelips, with riotous ornamentation.*

Montacute Somerset: *Count of Mortain (his castle).* 🏠 Montacute House, built of Ham Hill stone.

Meare Somerset: *Glastonbury Church. 3 fisheries, vineyard.* 🏠 Iron Age lake village, now on its own 'island' above the moors; 14th-century Fish House; manor house, once the summer retreat of the Abbots of Glastonbury.

Mells Somerset: *Glastonbury Church and Bishop of Coutances and Godiva, whose husband was the pre-Conquest holder, from the church. Mill.* 🏠 Beautiful Tudor manor house, seat of the Horne family, one of whom was 'little Jack Horner' of the nursery rhyme. 4 prehistoric camps nearby: Wadbury, Tedbury, Newbury and Kingsdown.

Market Drayton Shropshire: *William Pantulf from Earl Roger.* Town with fine 18th-century buildings; well known for the manufacture of horse-hair for chairs in the 19th century.

Malmesbury Wiltshire: *King's land, Malmesbury Abbey; Glastonbury Abbey and various landholders. Mill.* Town, a weaving centre until the 18th century. King Athelstan, who founded the hospital, was buried here 1000 years ago; the Normans built Malmesbury Abbey on the spot.

Mistley Essex: *Henry's wife from Roger de Raismes.* 🏠 A memorial tablet in the church to Richard Rigby, Paymaster of the Forces 1768–84, does not mention that he died leaving 'nearly half a million pounds of public money' that he had stolen.

MALHAM: *Monks Bridge, once used by monastic flocks of sheep.*

Malham West Riding, Yorkshire: *King's land; William de Percy.* ⊞ Popular walking and climbing centre on the Pennine Way; impressive limestone rock-faces at Gordale Scar and Malham Cove; Malham Tarn, a bird sanctuary. Charles Kingsley wrote *The Water Babies* (1863) at Malham Tarn House.

Milton Regis Kent: *King's land. 6 mills, 27 salt-houses, 32 fisheries. A due of 56½ weys of cheese was paid in Newington.* Suburb of Pittingbourne; church has some Saxon masonry.

Madeley Shropshire: *Church of St Milburga before and after 1066.* Town with a grange built by the priors of Much Wenlock, probably in the 13th century. It was a thriving iron-manufacturing centre in the 19th century, and home of the industrialist Abraham Darby from 1709 until his death in 1717.

Mannington Norfolk: *King's land, in the custody of Godric; William de Warenne. 2 mills. 40 goats.* ⊞ 18th-century Mannington Hall, part restored by the author Horatio Walpole.

Melbourne Derbyshire: *King's land. Church, mill.* Small town with a great pool, 12th-century tithe barn, hall with formal gardens and Norman church in its lower 'village'.

MELBOURNE: *The imposing nave of St Michael-with-St-Mary, with its 2 storeys of Norman arches. It probably stands on the site of the Domesday church.*

Nuneham Courtenay, Oxfordshire

Navestock Essex: *Canons of St Paul's; Ralph from Hamo the Steward. 4 beehives.* Norman church with memorials to Waldegrave family; James Waldegrave was Prime Minister for 5 days (8–12 June 1757).

Newbold Astbury Cheshire: *Gilbert Hunter from Earl Hugh.* Now Astbury. The church was granted to St Werburgh in the 11th century and rebuilt in the 13th and 16th centuries. The remains of Astbury Yew are possibly pre-1066. Nearby is Newbold, on the edge of Congleton.

Northey Island Essex: *Richard from Hamo the Steward; Hamo the Steward.* Island in estuary from which Viking invaders successfully fought Byrhtnoth's Anglo-Danish defence force.

> Richard de Courcy holds NUNEHAM (COURTENAY) from the King . . . 35 villagers with 3 fishermen have 14 ploughs; they pay 30s. 7 slaves; a mill at 20s; meadow, 40 acres; pasture . . . copse . . . Value before 1066, later and now £13. Hakon held it.

Nuneham had many owners between 1086 and the eighteenth century. Its poorish soils on the Lower Greensand produced a woodland attractive only to landscapers. When the Harcourts moved here from the dull vale of the Upper Thames they had no difficulty in making a cheap buy. Lord Harcourt didn't wait for the Duke of Marlborough to finish his new mansion, which was keeping the Headington quarries fully occupied. He had the stones of his house at Stanton Harcourt shipped down the Thames in barges. The former village green was planted with trees and its pond transformed into a curving lake with water pumped up from the Thames. Twenty years later the second Earl of Harcourt (the first had been drowned in a well, rescuing his dog) employed Capability Brown, who 'broke the whole prospect enjoyed from the house and the walks into a series of vistas with hanging woods, featuring the windings of the river [and] the spire of Abingdon Church . . .'

Today the house is owned by Oxford University and is used as a business conference centre. Brown's landscape, although still identifiable, looks somewhat plucked. The chapel is closed and part of the park has been sold to the Admiralty. Lock Cottage has fallen down and the seventeenth-century Old Barn Farmhouse was destroyed by troops encamped in the park before D-Day.

Despite all this, a certain magic still lingers in the first earl's new church which combines remoteness, austerity and the grandeur of a royal court.

Noke Oxfordshire: *Robert, Roger and Reginald from Earl William.*  Church built by William I's daughter, Gundrada.

Nunwell Hampshire: *King's land.* Parkland; Nunwell Farm and Trail. A skeleton of one of the Beaker people was found here.

Northbourne Kent: *St Augustine's Abbey.* Seaside. Northbourne Court is on the site of a grange built by St Augustine's monks.

Newport Essex: *King's land. 2 mills. 79 pigs.* On the Roman road to Cambridge; church with 700-year-old portable altar on which are the earliest-known English oil paintings on wood.

Ness Cheshire: *Walter de Vernon.* Part of Neston; birthplace of Lady Hamilton (1761–1815).

NUNEHAM COURTENAY: *A tranquil Thames-side scene; Horace Walpole believed it was one of the world's most beautiful landscapes.*

NORTON: *12th-c. doorway from the Augustinian priory.*

Norton Cheshire: *Ansfrid from William FitzNigel.* Wooded area on the outskirts of Runcorn; remains of Norton Priory.

Northwich Cheshire: *Earl Hugh. Salt-house.* Town that still produces salt; damaged by subsidence from saltmining. There is a medieval motte and bailey on Castle Hill.

Nantwich Cheshire: *William Malbank. Salt-pit, salt-pans.* Town, largely rebuilt (with the help of Elizabeth I) after a fire in 1583. Still has many black-and-white houses. Salt production from the *Domesday* pit continued until 1856.

North Curry Somerset: *King's land, formerly Earl Harold, with Bishop Maurice holding the church; Ansger le Breton from Count of Mortain. Fishery, vineyard. 20 cattle, 20 pigs, 100 sheep.*

NORTH LEIGH: *Windmill, possibly on its original* Domesday *site.*

North Leigh Oxfordshire: *Godfrey from Roger d'Ivry. Mill.* Windmill; Saxon church; remains of a Roman villa nearby.

Newington Bagpath Gloucestershire: *Roger from the king.* The last 2 men hanged for highway robbery are buried here.

Naunton Gloucestershire: *Robert D'Oilly, Cwenhild the nun from the king. Mill.* Just one long street; 15th-century dovecote with 1000 openings.

Nottingham Nottinghamshire: *King's land; Hugh FitzBaldric; the Sheriff; Roger de Bully; William Peverel; Ralph de Buron; Wulfbert; Ralph FitzHubert; Geoffrey Aselin; Richard Frail. Church.* Thriving, modern county town, traditionally renowned for its lace. Its imposing castle, now a museum, is on a post-Conquest site.

Newnham Gloucestershire: *William FitzBaderon.* Little town on the River Severn; mostly Georgian houses, some with old rope-walks down to the river.

Norton Malreward Somerset: *Wulfeva from Bishop of Coutances. Mill.* Hauteville's Quoit, a single stone forming part of a Bronze Age complex, nearby.

Nuneaton Warwickshire: *Earl Aubrey; Robert d'Oilly from Thorkell of Warwick. Mill.* Market town, once a Saxon settlement at the edge of the Forest of Arden. 'Nun' was added in 1290 when a Benedictine nunnery was established.

Nunburnholme East Riding, Yorkshire: *King's land; Forne FitzSigulf from the king.* Norman church with an Anglo-Saxon cross, c.1000.

NUNBURNHOLME: *Cross in 2 fragments.*

Olney, Buckinghamshire

The Bishop [of Coutances] holds OLNEY himself ... 24 villagers with 5 smallholders have 7 ploughs. 5 slaves; 1 mill at 40s and 200 eels; meadow for 10 ploughs; woodland, 400 pigs. In total, value £12; when acquired £7; before 1066 £12. Burgred held this manor; 1 Freeman, his man, had 1½ virgates; he could sell.

The present mill is probably on the site of the *Domesday* original. The 200 eels demanded as part of the rent were no doubt caught in traps, as no fishery is mentioned. The manorial woodland in which the pigs rooted would have been part of Yardley Chase.

In 1194 Olney passed from the king to the Earl of Chester and then to other families. By 1237 Olney had become a borough with its own tri-weekly courts. The Monday market, first mentioned in 1205/6, still exists. The town's hilarious Shrove Tuesday pancake race, said to be 500 years old, is heralded by the 'pancake bell'. The ladies, all Olney residents, must wear skirts and aprons with scarves or hats as they run the 400-yard course to the church porch, tossing their sizzling pancakes as they go. The pancakes that survive the race are given to the bellringer, who pays with a kiss.

John Newton was curate from 1764 to 1779. He had gone to sea at eleven years old. Eventually he became a slave-trader, a profession he abandoned as religious convictions grew. He convinced William Cowper, the poet, to move to Olney in 1767 believing that practical evangelical work would help the young, unstable man. During nearly 20 years at Orchard Side, in the Market Place, Cowper taught in the Sunday school, attended Newton's prayer meetings and nurtured his greenhouse exotica, which included pineapples.

With Newton, Cowper wrote the *Olney Hymns* (published in 1779), among which are 'Amazing Grace' and 'God Moves in a Mysterious Way'. In the garden of Orchard Side (now the Cowper and Newton Museum) the 'nutshell of a summerhouse' that served as the 'verse manufactory' survives.

Today, as in Cowper's time, the town has a quietly dignified character, with many modest Georgian stone façades (especially near the elegant stone bridge) and a magnificent church, which has one of only two medieval spires in Buckinghamshire.

OTHAM: *15th-century doorway with carved stone decoration.*

Otham Kent: *Geoffrey de Rots from Bishop of Bayeux.* 🏠 Picturesque; 15th-century yeoman's house.

Osmotherley North Riding, Yorkshire: *King's land.* 🏠 Stone houses; a mile north is the start of Lyke Wake Walk across 40 miles of the North York moors.

OLNEY: *View of the church across the River Ouse.*

OAKHAM: *The castle's Great Hall was built in the 12th c. and its fortifications still stand. The Domesday hall was probably timber.*

Oxborough Norfolk: *Godric the steward; Ralph de Limésy. 2 mills, fishery. 180 sheep.* ⊞ Fenland. Oxburgh Hall, a fine 15th-century moated mansion, is still occupied by its founders, the Bedingfield family.

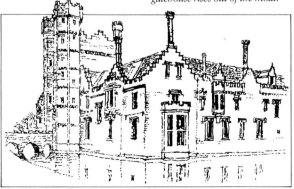

OXBOROUGH: *Oxburgh Hall's gatehouse rises out of the moat.*

Oakham Rutland: *King's land, with Albert the clerk holding the church. Church.* Small market town. Inside its Great Hall is a collection of horseshoes, said to have been donated by every king, queen and peer who has visited Oakham.

Overton Lancashire: *King's land.* ⊞ Church with Anglo-Saxon cornerstones, a Norman doorway and Norman walls.

Otford Kent: *Archbishop of Canterbury. 8 mills.* ⊞ Ruins of Otford Castle, the Archbishop of Canterbury's manor, where Thomas à Becket stayed. The castle was given to Henry VIII by Archbishop Cranmer.

Oadby Leicestershire: *Roger from Hugh de Grandmesnil; Countess Judith and Robert from her.* Part of Leicester; site of a pagan Anglo-Saxon cemetery.

Oakley Northamptonshire: *Lancelin from Countess Judith.* Now 2 villages of Great and Little Oakley, facing each other across quarries.

Oxford Oxfordshire: *King's land (royal borough), also various landholders and burgesses holding 243 dwellings.* University city, allegedly founded as a nunnery by Frideswide (d. 735). The first college, University College, dates from 1249. The city was the Royalist headquarters during the Civil War.

Ossington Nottinghamshire: *Ralph de Buron.* ⊞ Secluded; seat of the Denison family since 1768; hall demolished in 1963.

OSSINGTON: *The Denison monument to Robert, d. 1785.*

Perranzabuloe, Cornwall

The Canons of St Piran's hold PERRANZABULOE; before 1066 it was always free. 3 h[ides]. Land for 8 ploughs; 2 ploughs there; 2 slaves. 4 villagers and 8 smallholders. Pasture, 10 acres. 8 cattle; 30 sheep. Value 12s; value when the Count received it, 40s. Two lands have been taken from this manor which before 1066 paid four weeks' revenue to the Canons and 20s. to the Dean by custom. Berner holds one of them from the Count of Mortain; the Count has taken away all the stock from the other hide, which Odo holds from St Piran's.

Perranzabuloe was held by the collegiate church of St Piran, but as *Domesday* shows, the acquisitive Count of Mortain never missed an opportunity to enlarge his territory. Perranzabuloe has moved twice, and the reason is given in its name, which means Piran-in-the-sand. The Celtic missionary Piran apparently came from Ireland early in the sixth century and founded a monastery on the coast some two miles from the site of the present church. Legend has it that he floated across on a millstone, which may be a reference to the small stone altars such missionaries often carried.

The earliest church we can precisely locate – a building only about 25 feet by 12 – dates from the ninth century. The place where it stood can still be seen on the beach. It was excavated by a Truro antiquarian named Mitchell in 1835, who found all four walls intact and a highly ornamented doorway embellished with stone heads.

'The masonry of the building', he wrote, 'is of the rudest kind, and evidently of remote antiquity. There is not the slightest attempt at regular courses, but the stones, consisting of granite, quartz, sandstone, porphyry, etc., appear to have been thrown together almost at random …'

He recorded that many bodies lay buried within the chancel and the nave, and that several skeletons lay with their feet under the altar. One was a giant – some seven feet six inches tall.

'On the southern and western sides of this venerable ruin', he went on, 'is the ancient burying-ground, strewed over tens of thousands of human bones and teeth as white as snow …'

Unfortunately, nothing was done to protect the site. Local children knocked down the walls; souvenir hunters filched the stones, and the carved heads were carted off to be exhibited in the Truro Museum. Worst of all, according to the renowned antiquarian, the Rev. Sabine Baring-Gould, was 'the mischievous meddlesomeness of the curate-in-charge, Rev. William Haslam, who turned the altar stones about, as he had got a theory into his head that they had formed a tomb, and rebuilt them in this fashion, pointing east and west, and cut upon the altar-slab the words *S. Piranus*'. Haslam also claimed Mitchell's discoveries for his own.

The little church had been abandoned in the twelfth century because of the encroaching sand, and a new one was built some quarter of a mile inland beyond a stream. It stood safe for some 400 years. Then tin-miners in the area diverted the stream's flow for their own uses and the sand poured in once more. Some repairs were made early in the eighteenth century, but they didn't last, and in 1804 a third (or perhaps fourth) church was built. It stands at Lambourne on the main road, on land given by the local member of Parliament.

This, the present St Piran, incorporates fragments of its predecessor: the font; some wood carvings and window tracery, and parts of the tower. But nothing remains of the little church of Piran-in-the-Sands. For 750 years after *Domesday* it survived intact, most of it embalmed in sand; but when once more it saw the light of day, it was torn to pieces.

PANGBOURNE: *Village sign.*

Pangbourne Berkshire: *King's land; William from Miles Crispin. Mill.* ⊞ On the River Thames; toll gate on bridge. Kenneth Grahame, author of *The Wind In The Willows*, lived at Church Cottage.

Portesham Dorset: *Abbotsbury Abbey; the wife of Hugh FitzGrip.* ⊞ 17th-century manor house, home of Admiral Hardy who was present when Nelson died at the battle of Trafalgar.

Padstow Cornwall: *St Petroc's Church from St Michael's Church.* Fishing town with narrow slate alleys and quays. Padstow is named for St Petroc, who founded a monastery here in the 6th century.

PADSTOW: *Abbey House, possibly once part of a nunnery.*

Peasemore Berkshire: *Count of Evreux; Richard from Gilbert de Bretteville; Odelard from Ralph de Mortimer.* ⊞ Saxon settlement, with a church dedicated to St Peada. The manor house was once owned by Geoffrey Chaucer's son.

Pebmarsh Essex: *18 freemen from Richard FitzGilbert; Warengar from Roger Bigot; Leofcild from Richard FitzGilbert; Aubrey de Vere's wife.* ⊞ Courtauld's 1st silk mill started here (1798). Sir Ronald Storr, Governor of Jerusalem and Judea from 1917, is buried in the church.

Purleigh Essex: *Count Eustace; Hugh de Montfort; Richard from Robert Gernon; Walter the Deacon. 7 cobs, 306 sheep, 23 goats.* ⊞ Hilltop. Lawrence Washington, great-great-grandfather of George Washington, preached in its church.

PILTON: *Church screen with tracery unique in Devon.*

PRINCETOWN (**near Lydford**), Devonshire: *The prison churchyard reflects the town's gloomy history. The gaol, specially built in the early 19th century, replaced Lydford Castle as a prison. Lydford, a* Domesday *settlement, was held by the king and Ralph de Pomeroy in 1086.*

Purse Caundle Dorset: *Saeward from the king; Athelney Abbey; Alfred the butler.* ⊞ 15th-century Purse Caundle Manor. An earlier house was given by King John to John Alleyn who looked after sick or injured royal hounds.

Papplewick Nottinghamshire: *William Peverel.* ⚲ Cave, said to be Robin Hood's stable. Papplewick Hall, designed by the Adam brothers, was owned by John Walter, proprietor of *The Times.* The first English steam-powered mill was built here in 1785.

Pilton Devonshire: *Bishop of Coutances. Cob.* Part of Barnstaple.

Painswick Gloucestershire: *Roger de Lacy and Cirencester Church. 4 mills.* Small 'wool' town with many fine 17th-century and Georgian houses; mill; a hill called Paradise; Adam and Eve inn.

Papworth Cambridgeshire: *Count Alan; William from Richard FitzGilbert; Gilbert de Ghent; Payne from Hardwin of Scales; Eustace of Huntingdon and Walter and Ordnoth, the pre-Conquest holder, from him; Picot of Cambridge.* ⊞ Now 2 villages, Papworth Everard and Papworth St Agnes. Sir Thomas Malory, author of *Morte d'Arthur*, died in St Agnes in the 15th century.

Pendleton Lancashire: *Roger de Bully; Albert Grelley.* ⊞ On the edge of Pendle Moor. Pendle Hill was famous for its witches in the 17th century.

Pudsey West Riding, Yorkshire: *Ilbert de Lacy.* Town. Industries include textiles, engineering and tanning; birthplace of the cricketers Len Hutton and Herbert Sutcliffe.

PAINSWICK: *Typical of the Cotswolds: stone walls, stone-tiled roofs, steep-pitched gables.*

Quy Cambridgeshire: *Picot from Abbot of Ely; Reginald from Aubrey de Vere; Picot of Cambridge. 3 mills.* ⊞ Water mill on Quy Water. A mid-19th century hall stands on the site of the old village. The new village is Stow-cum-Quy.

Ribchester, Lancashire

Land of the King in Yorkshire . . .
Amounderness.
In Preston, Earl Tosti, 6c. taxable. These lands belong there. Ashton 2c., Lea 1c. [a list of 59 towns follows, including RIBCHESTER 2c.] All these villages and 3 churches belong to Preston. 16 of them have a few inhabitants, but how many is not known. The rest are waste. Roger de Poitou had them.

The River Ribble meanders unhurriedly to its meeting with the Irish Sea. Ribchester is poised on its north bank.

In *Domesday*, it belonged to that sad region called Amounderness, where 46 of 62 settlements were deserted and waste. After brutally suppressing rebellions in the East and West Ridings of Yorkshire in 1069–70, King William had moved south-west to overrun the entire county and to debauch upon Amounderness, which was treated with almost as great severity as Yorkshire. Ribchester, which lay on a major route to the west coast, was unlikely to have escaped his attentions.

In Roman days this had been *Bremetennacum Veteranorum*, the largest fort in Lancashire, at the junction of roads to Chester, York and Carlisle. Five hundred cavalrymen were stationed here, and there was a substantial community of veterans, who ended their days as farmers or horse breeders in this remote outpost.

Unhappily next to nothing is known about Ribchester's history for 1000 years. The few discoveries show that Saxons probably lived within the abandoned shell of the Roman town.

Ribchester was again reduced to ruins by the Scots in 1323, but signs of its Roman past still remained. 'Great squarid stones, voultes and antique coins be found ther,' wrote John Leland, Henry VIII's travelling antiquary. A Roman museum displays many small items uncovered by successive excavations, the foundations of two garrison granaries and a western defensive ditch. There is little to confirm a wistful local saying:
It is written upon a wall in Rome:
Ribchester was as rich as any town in Christendom.

Radcliffe on Trent
Nottinghamshire: *Fredegis and Wulfgeat from William Peverel; Walter d'Aincort; ½ fishery, ⅓ fishery.* Town opposite Nottingham on the River Trent. Henry VII heard mass here before leading his army to defeat his enemies at East Stoke in 1487.

REPTON: *Saxon crypt beneath St Wystan Church.*

Repton Derbyshire: *King's land. Church, 2 mills.* ⊞ Mercian capital in the 7th century. Repton public school, founded *c.*1556, incorporates the remains of a 12th-century priory.

Roydon (near Diss) Norfolk: *Walter from Robert Malet; St Edmund's; Hugh from Ralph de Beaufour. 2 horses at the hall. 30 pigs.* ⊞ Home of Sir Henry Bartle Frere (1815–84), who negotiated the suppression of the Zanzibar slave trade.

Raynham Norfolk: *King's land, in the custody of Godric; Roger Bigot; Reynald Fitzlvo and Boteric from him; Hugh de Montfort. 3 mills, salt-house.* Now 2 villages, East Raynham, home of Charles 'Turnip' Townsend (1674–1738) who introduced the turnip to England and West Raynham.

Rugeley Staffordshire: *King's land. Mill.* Industrial town, home of William Palmer, The Rugeley Poisoner, a 19th-century doctor who turned to murder to pay his gambling debts.

Reculver Kent: *Archbishop of Canterbury. Church, mill, 5 salt-houses, fishery.* Seaside town; site of the Roman fortress Regulbium. The twin towers of ruined St Mary's Church were built by the Normans on the site of a 7th-century Saxon church and are used as a landmark by ships.

Rochdale Lancashire: *Roger de Poitou.* Important cotton manufacturing town where the Co-operative Movement began in 1844.

RIPPLE: *15th-c. misericords in Ripple church. 16 stalls of the 15th c.*

Redbourne Lincolnshire: *King's land; Bishop of Lincoln and the Canons of St Mary; Ivo Tailboirs; Colsuan; Gocelin FitzLanbert; Osbern d'Arcis; Odo the Arblaster; Heppo the Arblaster. Mill.* ⊞ Hall once the home of the Dukes of St Albans, descendants of Nell Gwynn.

Rudyard Staffordshire: *King's land.* ⊞ The architect, J.L. Kipling, got engaged here and named his son Rudyard after the spot.

Ripple Worcestershire: *Worcester Church. Mill.* ⊞ Norman church on a Saxon site.

Radwinter Essex: *Richard from Eudo the Steward; Demiblanc from Aubrey de Vere; Guthred from Tihel le Breton; Frodo, brother of Abbot Baldwin. 8 beehives. 18 cattle, 30 goats.* ⊞ Its Old Rectory was the home of William Harrison (rector 1559–93), commentator on 16th-century morals and mores.

Riddlesden West Riding, Yorkshire: *King's land.* East and West Riddlesden Halls are 17th century. The last three Murgatroyds, owners of the East Hall, ended up in York Debtor's Prison in the reign of Charles II; fine timbered barn.

RIBCHESTER: *The River Ribble flows as peacefully now as it did when the Romans were stationed here.*

Rochester Kent: *Bishop of Bayeux from Bishop of Rochester.* Ancient city now a major port and an industrial and commercial centre. Rochester Cathedral, begun in 1077, was completed in the 13th century. Rochester Castle, built in 1127, has the tallest keep in Britain.

Revesby Lincolnshire: *Ivo Tailbois. 2 churches (with East Kirkby).* Round barrows; home of the naturalist Sir Joseph Banks, who accompanied Captain Cook on his voyage around the world, 1768–71.

Rugby Warwickshire: *Edwulf from Thorkell of Warwick. Mill.* Market town; home of Rugby School.

Rousdon Devonshire: *Odo from the king, formerly Mathilda.* Victorian mansion imitating a variety of styles from Renaissance to Louis XIV, built for the Peek Frean family.

Rudford Gloucestershire: *Madog, the pre-Conquest holder, from the king. Mill.* A 20ft high obelisk was erected last century to mark where Welsh soldiers fell in the Civil War in 1643.

Rivenhall Essex: *Count Eustace; formerly Queen Edith; Clarenbold from Swein of Essex; Ascelin from Robert Gernon; Roger God-save-ladies. ½ mill, 4 beehives.* Rivenhall Place (16th and 18th centuries), was the home of Kitty O'Shea, whose husband named Charles Parnell as co-respondent when he filed for divorce.

Rochford Essex: *Alfred from Swein of Essex. Mill. 3 cobs, 2 foals, 160 sheep.* Market town. Rochford Hall was built for Sir Robert Rich, the 2nd Earl of Warwick, in the 17th century.

Ripon West Riding, Yorkshire: *Archbishop of York before and after 1066. Church, mill, fishery.* Market town with some light industry. Cathedral is 12th to 15th century, but there have been monasteries on the site since the 7th century. The Saxon crypt (AD 670) has a narrow passage called St Wilfrid's Needle, the ability to pass through it being a mark of chastity. 13th-century Wakeman's House; Wakeman's Horn still blown at 9.00 pm.

Rexworthy Somerset: *Robert from Roger de Courseulles.* Farm.

REXWORTHY: *Moated farmhouse; 'worthy' was the Saxon term for an isolated farm.*

Rushton Northamptonshire: *King's land; Grestain Abbey; Hugh from Robert de Tosny; William from Robert de Bucy; Eustace from Countess Judith. 2 mills.*  16th-century Triangular Lodge was built by Sir Thomas Tresham as a manifestation of his Roman Catholic faith.

Rothwell West Riding, Yorkshire: *Ilbert de Lacy. Mill.* Town. Coal-mining and chemicals. John Blenkinsop (1783–1831), the railway pioneer, is buried here.

Richmond North Riding, Yorkshire: *Enisan; Count Alan. Church, fishery.* Town, capital of Swaledale. Remains of 12th-century St Martin's Priory; market place; Georgian theatre; St Mary's church; imposing castle dating from the 11th century.

Raskelf North Riding, Yorkshire: *King's land.* Nearby moorland well known for rare orchids.

Rotherham West Riding, Yorkshire: *Nigel from Count of Mortain. Church.* Town. Industries are coal-mining, iron, steel, and glass. The fort at nearby Scholeswood is probably prehistoric. The boys of the Grammar School unsuccessfully helped to defend the bridge against Royalist troops in 1643.

Ratcliffe on the Wreak Leicestershire: *Robert Burdet's wife from Robert de Bucy. Mill.* Hall; old mill; birthplace of Richard Kilbye (1561–1620), one of the translators of the authorized version of the Bible.

Rolleston Nottinghamshire: *Archbishop of York; Bishop of Bayeux; Walter d'Aincourt. Mill, church.* On the River Greet; church with Saxon masonry and fragments of a Saxon cross; manorial earthworks; racecourse.

Rowington Warwickshire: *Roger from Hugh de Grandmesnil.* An early clearing in the Forest of Arden; Shakespeare Hall, home of the Shakespeare family, to whom, allegedly, the playwright was related.

Roxton Bedfordshire: *Rhiwallon from Hugh de Beauchamp; William Speke. Mill (260 eels).* The countryman's linen smock was initiated here in 1714.

Rockingham Northamptonshire: *King's land. Castle.* Castle, originally Norman, built on William I's orders.

ROCKINGHAM: *The vista from the terrace of the castle, with the church beneath its walls.*

Stow on the Wold, Gloucestershire

[Evesham Abbey] holds MAUGERSBURY near STOW (ON THE WOLD). Before 1066 there were 8 hides and a ninth hide lies near St Edward's Church. King Aethelred gave it, exempt. In lordship 3 ploughs; 12 villagers, 1 free man and a priest, who between them have 7 ploughs. 6 slaves; a mill at 8s; some meadow. Value before 1066, 100s; now £7.

> Stow on the Wold
> Where the wind blows cold
> and the cooks can't roast their dinners.

'Eduuardstou', the *Domesday* name for Stow on the Wold, almost certainly refers to Edward the Martyr, King of the English, whose final resting place was with the nuns at Shaftesbury. He was murdered at Corfe Castle in 978 by those who wished to see his half brother, Aethelred, made king. Aethelred probably granted land to the monks of Evesham as an act of reparation. The Abbot of Evesham received recognition of 'a port and market at Stow St Edwards' in 1107. Permission to hold two annual fairs followed in the reign of Edward III. The canonization of Edward the Confessor had taken place and the earlier St Edward the Martyr was eased out.

Stow prospered by being at a crossroads, but an advantage in peace became a liability in war, and when King and Parliament took up arms, Stow was caught between them. Sir Jacob Astley led the garrison of Worcester to reinforce the king, moving through Stow. The ensuing battle left 200 dead in the square. Forced to surrender, Astley is reputed to have said, 'You may now sit and play, for you have done all your work if you fall not out amongst yourselves.'

The Chamberlaynes (of Maugersbury) and the Leighs (of Addlestrop, three miles to the east of Stow) remained Stow's patrons and benefactors until the twentieth century. They were distinguished families: the Leighs produced a master of Balliol and Jane Austen, whose mother was a Leigh; and the Chamberlaynes produced John Chamberlayne, one of the first Fellows of the Royal Society (1702) and 200 years of naval officers. 'Make way for the Weights and Measures of Maugersbury,' Admiral Chamberlayne shouted as he ran up the aisle at the coronation of William IV, determined to secure a seat – an appropriate cry for a town of very pleasant shops and shopkeepers.

Saffron Walden Essex: *Geoffrey de Mandeville. Mill, 30 beehives.* Delightful town which specialized in growing saffron crocuses in the Middle Ages. Audley End, now a magnificent example of 17th-century architecture, was built on the ruins of a monastery founded by the Mandeville family.

Selby West Riding, Yorkshire: *Abbot of Selby from the Archbishop of York.* Ship-building port on the River Ouse with flour and mustard mills. It is believed to be the birthplace of Henry I (1068–1135), the Conqueror's only English-born son. The abbey church (built for the Benedictines established here in 1097) has fine Norman doorways. Selby coalfield is nearby.

Sandwich Kent: *Archbishop of Canterbury. 40,000 herrings.* Small town, one of the Cinque Ports. In 850 it was the landing place for one of the first Danish attacks on England, which led ultimately to Canute becoming king in 1016.

Sherborne Dorset: *Bishop of Salisbury, formerly Queen Edith.* 1000-year-old town, dominated by Sherborne Abbey.

SHERBORNE: *Edward I's coat-of-arms. He founded the boys' school that now occupies part of the abbey buildings.*

SANDWICH: *A cobbled lane leads up to this narrow 16-c. gatehouse.*

SKELTON: *13th-c. church carvings, probably by masons who built York Minster.*

Skelton (near Saltburn) North Riding, Yorkshire: *Richard from Count of Mortain.* Castle, 1794, built on the site of a Norman one; remains of old well and cross.

Scawton North Riding, Yorkshire: *Count of Mortain; Robert Malet.* The Hare Inn was supposed to be the smallest inn in England before living quarters were added.

Shifford Oxfordshire: *Columban from Bishop of Lincoln. Fishery (250 eels).* Saxon ford and earthworks. Alfred held one of the earliest parliaments on Court Close near the church, in the late 9th century.

Shrewton Wiltshire: *Edward of Salisbury and Godfrey and Theobald from him. Mill.* Bridge over the River Till. At the Blind House, shaped like a beehive, people were imprisoned before execution.

Stoke Poges Buckinghamshire: *Walter from William FitzAnsculf. Mill.* Thomas Gray's poem 'Elegy in a Country Churchyard' immortalized this village.

St Pauls Cray Kent: *Ansketel de Rots from Bishop of Bayeux. Mill.* Industrial, now part of Greater London. The 13th-century church is dedicated to St Paulinus, one of St Augustine's missionaries.

Somerleyton Suffolk: *King's land, kept by Roger Bigot; Ralph the Crossbowman. Church.* Built by Samuel M. Peto, a rich railway contractor, in the mid-19th century; ornamental cottages.

Swanscombe Kent: *Helto from Bishop of Bayeux. 6 fisheries.* Industrial district and site of Barnsfield Pit, which yielded the earliest fossilized human remains found in Britain. The old parish church has a Saxon tower.

Sulgrave Northamptonshire: *Hugh, Landric and Odbert from Giles brother of Ansculf.* The manor was owned by George Washington's family from 1540 to 1659; Church with Saxon doorway.

Sibthorpe Nottinghamshire: *Fredegis from Count Alan; Robert from William Peverel; Arngrim from Ilbert de Lacy. Church, 1¼ mills.* Easter Sepulchre in church; 20 Irish yew trees in graveyard, said to be 1000 years old; old manor house; traces of a moat; medieval dovecote, 98ft in circumference.

Stokesay Shropshire: *Roger de Lacy. Mill.* Fortified manor house built by Laurence de Ludlow, a wealthy clothier, in 1290. Undamaged by the Civil War, it is one of the finest examples of its kind in Britain.

Stoke sub Hamdon Somerset: *William de Mohun; Mauger from Count of Mortain. Mill.* Now 2 villages, East and West Stoke; below Ham Hill, with one of Britain's largest hill-forts, traces of a Roman villa, and stone quarries.

STOKE SUB HAMDON: *'Fives' stone wall, c. 1780.*

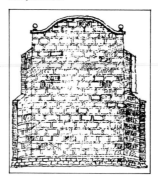

Snitterfield Warwickshire: *Count of Meulan.* Originally Neolithic; ancient Marroway road, along which the men of Mercia marched to attack to Wessex warriors. Richard Shakespeare, grandfather of William, farmed here.

Sole End Warwickshire: *Godric from Count of Meulan.* Mrs Ann Garner, one of the Dodson sisters in George Eliot's *The Mill on the Floss,* lived at Sole End Farm.

Stanmore Middlesex: *Count of Mortain; Roger de Raismes.* Part of London. Handel was organist at the church.

Stallingborough Lincolnshire: *Archbishop of York and Herbert from him; Bishop of Bayeux; Hugh FitzBaldric; Norman d'Arci. ½ church, 3½ mills, 2 sites, 4½ salt-pans, ½ slaughter-house.* The Mercian King Offa is thought to have held his court here 12 centuries ago. The church has a monument to Anne Askew, martyred at the stake in 1546 for nonconformity; she wanted a divorce.

Southwold Suffolk: *Abbot of St Edmund's. Moiety of sea weir, 25,000 herrings.* Little picturesque town on a cliff top with marshes behind, a prosperous fishing town until the sea began to close the harbour mouth in the late 16th century.

Springfield Essex: *Corp from Robert Gernon; Robert from Ranulf Peverel. Mill, beehive. 2 asses, 14 cobs, 5 foals, 26 cattle.* Part of Chelmsford; Roman-bricked Norman church. Oliver Goldsmith lived here.

Sprotbrough West Riding, Yorkshire: *King's land; Roger de Bully.* Sir Walter Scott is said to have lived here, gathering local colour for *Ivanhoe* (1819).

Selborne Hampshire: *King's land; Herbert from Walter FitzRoger. Church.* Home of the 18th-century naturalist Gilbert White, author of *Natural History of Selborne.* Its yew tree is believed to be 1000 years old.

SELBORNE: *The Wakes, Gilbert White's house.*

SALTWOOD: *Now a family home, the castle was once Hugh de Montfort's stronghold from where he controlled the Romney Marshes.*

Saltwood Kent: *Hugh de Montfort from Archbishop of Canterbury. Church. 9 mills.* Suburb of Hythe. Thomas à Becket's murderers are said to have plotted his death in the great hall of its castle.

St Albans Hertfordshire: *St Albans Church. Park for woodland beasts, fishpond.* Cathedral city, originally Verulamium, a key Roman settlement, destroyed by Boadicea. It was rebuilt and named after the first British martyr, the Roman soldier, Alban.

Singleton Sussex: *Earl Roger and Payne, Geoffrey, William and a monk of St Evroul's from him. 3 mills, church.* 🌳 Wooded; church with a Saxon tower.

Salford Lancashire: *Roger de Poitou.* Industrial town in the Manchester conurbation. Peel Park was the first free municipal library; the art gallery has paintings by L.S. Lowry (1887–1976).

Shelsley Worcestershire: *Walter from Ralph de Tosny; Osbern FitzRichard. 2 fisheries (16 sticks of eels).* Now 2 villages, Shelsley Walsh, whose part Norman church is limestone quarried from Southstone Rock, and Shelsley Beauchamp.

Studley Royal West Riding, Yorkshire: *Archil from William de Percy; Gospatric; Esnerbern, the pre-Conquest holder, from the king.* 🦌 Deer-park, outstanding 18th-century gardens, leading to the impressive ruins of Fountains Abbey, a 12th-century Cistercian foundation. Fountains Hall nearby dates from 1611.

STUDLEY ROYAL: (overleaf) *Fountains Abbey.*

Turvey, Bedfordshire

In TURVEY the Bishop [of Coutances] ... 3 villagers have 3 ploughs; 8 smallholders and 1 slave. 1 mill, 20s; meadow; woodland, 40 pigs. Value £6; when acquired 40s; before 1066 £6. 3 Freemen, King Edward's men, held this manor; they could sell and grant. The Bishop has this land in exchange for Bleadon, as his men state.

There are no less than eight *Domesday* entries for Turvey, but the most significant is that which describes the holding of the bishop of Coutances, whose manor was eventually to absorb most of the Turvey land held by others.

At some time before 1221 two de Alneto heiresses to Turvey, Alice and Sarah, married a Mordaunt and a Robert d'Ardres respectively. Though a d'Ardres had held Turvey land in 1086, it was as Mordaunt Manor that the two were united in the late fourteenth century.

The Mordaunts were a colourful and eccentric family. Edward Mordaunt, on the Sunday before a religious feast in 1372, killed his wife before drowning himself in a Turvey pool. Later Mordaunts achieved high rank in the Tudor courts. Henry Mordaunt, a fervent Catholic, was suspected of being implicated in the Gunpowder Plot and long imprisoned. His son was an ardent Parliamentarian in the Civil War, but *his* son, a celebrated Royalist, lost his Turvey estates for his allegiance. The manor passed from the family in 1786.

TURVEY: *The abbey harks back to the days of the Mordaunts.*

The Priory of St Neots benefited from gifts of Turvey land during the twelfth and thirteenth centuries and by 1278 had amassed 100 acres.

The village's most famous incumbent was Legh Richmond, rector from 1805 to 1827. Although he was a highly popular touring preacher and evangelist, eight volumes he compiled of selections from the Reformation divines proved unremunerative. He is buried in the churchyard.

Some masonry of the pre-Conquest church can still be seen in the upper parts of the north and south nave walls, but the Saxon chancel has been rebuilt. As in 1086, there is one mill, but most of the village was rebuilt in golden limestone during the mid-nineteenth century.

TOPSHAM: *View of the river estuary and out towards the sea.*

Taynton Gloucestershire: *William Goizenboded.* Scattered. Taynton House has a 1695 barn, cider-mill and oxhouse. Taynton stone was used to build Blenheim Palace.

TAYNTON:*Hown Hall, 18th-c. brick building.*

Topsham Devonshire: *King's land. Cob, 5 cattle, 50 sheep.* Small quayside town, once a centre for shipbuilding and allied trades.

Taunton Somerset: *Bishop of Winchester. 3 mills, market.* County town and commercial centre; 12th-century castle keep, with later additions. The Bloody Assizes were held here after Monmouth's Rebellion in 1685. 17th-century alms-houses.

Tolleshunt Essex: *Bishop of Bayeux; Count Eustace and Adelulf and St Martin's from him; Odo from Swein of Essex; Humphrey from Hugh de Montfort; Robert de Verly from Robert Gernon; Bernard from Ralph Baynard; Humphrey from Ranulf Peverel; Mauger from Robert FitzCorbucion; Gundwin. 13 salt-houses, 8 beehives. 560 sheep, 38 goats, 3 cobs, 2 cows, calf, 20 cattle.* Now 2 villages, Tolleshunt D'Arcy and Tolleshunt Major and hamlet of Tolleshunt Knight. The church of D'Arcy contains D'Arcy family treasure; a knight is carved in effigy in Tolleshunt Knights church. Tolleshunt Major takes its name from Mauger, the *Domesday* tenant.

Tattershall Thorpe
Lincolnshire: *Bishop of Durham; Bishop of Bayeux; Eudo FitzSpirwic. 2¼ mills, 12 fisheries.*

Temple Newsham West Riding, Yorkshire: *Ansfrid from Ilbert de Lacy.* Magnificent Tudor and Jacobean house in a Leeds park. Darnley, husband of Mary, Queen of Scots, is said to have been born here; 4 ghosts.

Totnes Devonshire: *Iudhael of Totnes.* Town, once a Saxon market centre with a mint; Saxon walls are still traceable and the ruins of a castle built by Iudhael remain.

TOTNES: *The castle, owned by a friend of William I, was mentioned in 1080, and restored in the 13th c.*

Tong Shropshire: *Earl Roger.*

TONG: *The church is filled with monuments, like this one to the Vernon family, 16th c.*

TATTERSHALL THORPE: *The near-by castle was built by Lord Cromwell in the 15th c. as a fine residence, with magnificent fireplaces.*

Tyburn Middlesex: *Barking Abbey before and after 1066.* Part of London. Criminals were executed here as early as 1196. Number 49 Connaught Square is said to be the site of the 17th-century gallows where the bodies of Cromwell, Ireton and Bradshaw were hung after disinterment.

Thornton (near Bradford) West Riding, Yorkshire: *Ilbert de Lacy.* District of Bradford. The Rev Patrick Brontë was the parson here and his 4 children were born at 74 Market Street (1816–20).

Tusmore Oxfordshire: *Thorold from Walter Giffard.* Tusmore House. Pope's *Rape of the Lock* (1712) was based on Lord Petre, a 20-year-old peer, who cut off one of the curls of a Tusmore belle, Arabella Fermor.

Tolpuddle Dorset: *Abbotsbury Abbey. 2 mills. 300 sheep..* Home of the Tolpuddle Martyrs, who formed the first trade union and were sentenced to transportation to Australia (1834).

Tapeley Devonshire: *Osbern from Bishop of Coutances. 10 cattle, 20 goats.* House once owned by John Christie, who founded Glyndebourne just after World War II.

Upton on Severn, Worcestershire

... the Bishop [of Worcester] also holds RIPPLE with 1 member UPTON (ON SEVERN) ... 2 priests who have 1½ hides with 2 ploughs; 40 villagers and 16 smallholders with 36 ploughs. 8 male slaves, 1 female. A mill; meadow, 30 acres; woodland ½ league long and 3 furlongs wide, in MALVERN (CHASE). From this he had honey and hunting and whatever came from there and 10s in addition. Now it is in the Forest. The Bishop receives from it pasture dues, firewood and (timber) for repairing houses. The value was and is £10.

If it were not for the pubs and the teashops and the exquisite Georgian police station, Upton could be some foreign resort. The slender church tower with its baroque copper dome has an un-English look, as do the little tiled pagoda huts around the yacht marina.

The expansion of the king's forest was a phenomenon that began with the Conqueror and continued throughout Henry I's reign. There is no *Domesday* reference to the river, which was probably already transporting timber, salt, wine and cider, as well as tiles and pottery made at nearby Hanley Castle.

The symbol of Upton's prosperity might well be the two-masted trow that employed sail – and, below Gloucester, the tide – as well as gangs of 'bow halliers' where the river needed help, which may explain the town's former rowdy reputation. In 1832, they rioted in protest at horses being used on the towpath. Court records abound with references to river pirates and to the casting of gigantic nets by Upton men to haul in so many salmon that communities upstream were in uproar.

Upton had severe problems by the 1650s: 'We do order yt no Cowes Bellys be emptied in the streets by ye buchers', and '... no person within the Berrow shall suffer any Mixon (dungheap) to lye above the space of 16 days.' With sawpits in the main street, pigsties on the bridge, and an overflowing gumstool (ducking pond) at the bottom of New Street, it is not surprising that Upton was swept by epidemics: plague in 1665, recurrent smallpox, and a cholera outbreak in 1832 which, at its height, killed 50 people in a month.

Once the railway arrived, the barge quays emptied and, as if to signal the end of an era, Upton Old Bridge fell down in the floods of 1852. Upton hardly knows any more that it is on the Severn. The absence of any mention of the river in *Domesday* was perhaps a premonition.

Ulverston Lancashire: *Thorulf from the king.* Town with a Tudor church and many Quaker associations. The tower on Hoad Hill, a copy of the Eddystone Lighthouse, is a memorial to the founder of the Royal Geographical Society, Sir John Barrow (1764–1848).

Uffcott Wiltshire: *Roger from Durand of Gloucester; Wulfric, formerly his father, from the king.* By an ancient ridgeway; Barbury Castle, a prehistoric hill-fort where the West Saxons beat the Britons in the Battle of Beranburh, AD 556.

Ugglebarnby North Riding, Yorkshire: *Earl Hugh and William de Percy from him.* Hillside; the Lord of Ugglebarnby led the hunters whose murder of a hermit for protecting a boar about 1160 led to the yearly penance of 'Planting the Penny Hedge' in Whitby.

Upper Penn Staffordshire: *William FitzAnsculf and Robert from him.* Mill. Base of a preaching cross, reputedly set up by Lady Godiva in 1050.

UPTON ON SEVERN: *No more lovely scene could be imagined than this distant view of the village, its 'oriental' church tower and dome silhouetted against the Malvern Hills and the Worcestershire Beacon.*

Wath upon Dearne, Wentworth, West Riding, Yorkshire

Woolston (in Wistanstow) Shropshire: *Picot from Earl Roger.*

WINSTER: *Market Hall with 17th-c. arches.*

Wythemail Northamptonshire: *Fulchere from Walter the Fleming.* Wythemail Park Farm with part of a moat was perhaps the old manor house.

Witchford Cambridgeshire: *Abbot of Ely.* Thurstan, Ely's last Saxon abbot, was born here, and the monks of Ely met the Conqueror here to make their submission.

WILLINGALE: *2 Norman churches in one churchyard.*

In WATH (UPON DEARNE) ... Roger [de Bully] and 4 villagers and 8 smallholders with 1 plough. Value before 1066, 40s; now 10s. To this manor belongs jurisdiction in SWINTON and WENTWORTH.... This land is waste. Woodland pasture, 14 furlongs long and 5 wide.

The name Wath upon Dearne means 'ford on the River Dearne'. Wath had declined in value since the Conquest but only the holdings at Swinton and Wentworth were described as waste. Wentworth, a neighbouring village, which was in the soke of de Bully's manor, was probably largely woodland; by 1303, however, a farm called Wentworth Woodhouse had been established.

This is the name given today to one of the grandest of English stately homes. The house, which has two contrasting fronts, was built between 1725 and 1750 for Thomas Wentworth, the first marquis of Rockingham. The ambitious 600ft east façade designed by Henry Flitcroft is the longest in England.

Until the 1800s the great fortune and ability of the Wentworths and their successors, the Fitzwilliams, enabled them to control the political life of Yorkshire and to some extent that of the country. Charles, the second marquis of Rockingham, was twice prime minister and he and his father erected various 'follies' on the estate expressing their Whig political views, now threatened by neglect and subsidence caused by nearby mining.

Coal-mining had begun by the late fourteenth century, but the greatest wealth came in the nineteenth century with the sinking of the 'Main' collieries.

Although Wath upon Dearne had had a market charter in 1312, it remained largely an agricultural village until the opening of the Dearne and Dove Canal in 1797. Today both Wath manors are predominantly industrial.

Widford Hertfordshire: *Bishop of London and Theodbert from him. Mill.* John Elliot of Widford preached the Gospel to the Red Indians. His psalm book was the first book printed in America.

Willingale Doe and Spain Essex: *Hervey from Count Alan; Warner from Swein of Essex; Ravenot from Ranulf Peverel; Adam son of Durand Malzor. 5 beehives.* Once 2 villages, Willingale Doe and Willingale Spain, named after Norman lords d'Eu and d'Epaignes. Their churches stand side by side.

White Waltham Berkshire: *Bishop of Durham, formerly Chertsey Abbey. Church.* Church with Norman carvings. Arthur Tudor, Henry VIII's son, lived at Waltham Place.

Winster Derbyshire: *Cola from Henry de Ferrers.* Market since 1640; lead-mining in the 18th century. A Pancake Race takes place every Shrove Tuesday.

Wednesbury Staffordshire: *King's land. Mill.* Industrial town surrounded by rivers and canals. St Bartholomew's Church on the hilltop was once the site of a heathen temple to Woden. A battle is said to have been fought there between Britons and Saxons, in AD 592.

Westmill Hertfordshire: *Ansketel from Robert Gernon; Roger from Ralph de Tosny. 4 mills.* Thatched cottage belonged to Charles Lamb; museum of Westmill relics dating back to Roman times.

Watton Hertfordshire: *Ansketel from Archbishop of Canterbury; Westminster Abbey, Godwin from Count Alan; Derman and Alfward from the king.* Now Watton at Stone. Watton Hall was rebuilt in 1636; an inscription reads: 'Watton Hall alias Watkins Hall'.

WHITE WALTHAM: *Double stocks made of oak.*

Wootton Rivers Wiltshire: *King's land, formerly Queen Edith, with Mont St Michel holding the 2 churches.* On the Kennet and Avon Canal. The church clock was made out of old prams and bedsteads by Mr Jack Spratt, to commemorate George V's Coronation (1911).

Woolston (in West Felton) Shropshire: *Rainald the Sheriff from Earl Roger.* St Winifred's well marks spot where the saint's body rested on its way from Holywell to Shrewsbury.

Ware Hertfordshire: *Hugh de Grandmesnil. 5 mills, park for woodland beasts, vines. 375 eels.* Town, known to the Danes who brought their ships up the River Lea.

Whitchurch Hampshire: *Bishop of Winchester. 3 mills, church.* Small market town, called after a pre-Conquest white church. A silk mill on an island in the river is one of only about 3 operating in England.

WHITCHURCH: *The busy Domesday village is now a rural peaceful scene.*

Wombourn Staffordshire: *Ralph from William FitzAnsculf. 2 mills.* Town. A church is dedicated to St Benedict Biscop (b. AD 628), said to have introduced glass windows to England.

Woodham Mortimer Essex: *Ranulf Peverel.*  Hall where Dr Peter Chamberlain, Physician in Ordinary to James I, Charles I and Charles II, lived.

Wingham Kent: *Archbishop of Canterbury. 2 mills, fishery, salthouse.* Set among woodland. Next to the medieval Old Canonry is an 18th-century house built on the site of the archbishop's manor house.

WHARRAM PERCY (overleaf): *The Domesday settlement in this quiet dip of the Yorkshire hills may not have looked very different from the landscape we see today.*

Wharram Percy East Riding, Yorkshire: *King's land and Gilbert from the king.* Cottage; ruined church; earthworks of deserted village.

Walton Suffolk: *Roger Bigot and Norman, the pre-Conquest holder, from him; Abbot of Ely and Hervey Beruarius from him; Hugh de Montfort. Church, mill. 146 sheep.* Merged with Felixstowe in 1895; submerged ruins of a Roman fortress. It may be the site of St Felix's See of Dommoc.

WESTON-UNDER-LIZARD: *The Temple of Diana by James Paine.*

Weston-under-Lizard
Staffordshire: *Reginald de Balliol.* ⊞ By Watling Street. Hall. The park was landscaped by Capability Brown in the 18th century.

Wellingborough
Northamptonshire: *Norigot from Bishop of Coutances; Crowland Abbey; Hugh and Gilbert from Countess Judith. 3 mills.* Victorian brick-built town, a centre of footwear and clothing industries. Earlier buildings include the largely Jacobean Croyland Abbey. Mills.

WELLINGBOROUGH: *The nave ceiling of St Mary's church, begun 1908.*

Waltham Holy Cross Essex: *Bishop of Durham. 3 mills, 5 fisheries, 12 London houses, gate.* London district, including Waltham Abbey. Possibly the best of the 12 Eleanor crosses that marked the route of Queen Eleanor's funeral procession from Nottingham to London was built here.

Wrington Somerset: *Glastonbury Church and Roger de Courseulles and Saewulf, the pre-Conquest holder, from the church. 3 mills. 46 cattle, 30 pigs, 278 sheep.* ⊞ Birthplace of the philosopher John Locke (1632–1704).

Woolsthorpe Lincolnshire: *Robert de Tosny. Church, 4½ mills.* ⊞ Birthplace of Sir Isaac Newton (1642–1727).

West Monkton Somerset: *Glastonbury Church and Bishop of Winchester, Roger de Courseulles and Serlo de Burcy from the church.* ⊞ Almshouse, once a leper hospital, rebuilt by the Abbot of Glastonbury 1510–1515.

Weybourne Norfolk: *Ranulf from Earl Hugh. 2 mills. 10 cattle, 36 goats.* ⊞ On the coast; Saxon church tower. The deeply shelving beach was heavily defended from 1588 to 1939, for 'He that would old England win/ Must at Weybourne Hope begin.'

Whitby North Riding, Yorkshire: *Earl Hugh and William de Percy from him.* Town, resort and small port; fishing and boat-building. The boyhood home of Captain Cook (1728–79) is preserved; remains of the 13th-century abbey are on the site of the abbey of 657, which was destroyed by the Danes in 867.

West Witton North Riding, Yorkshire: *Count Alan.* ⊞ In Wensleydale, on the northern slope of Penhill; custom of 'Burning Owd Bartle' in effigy on the Saturday after St Bartholomew's Day is thought to commemorate the fate of a local thief.

Wattisfield Suffolk: *Earl Hugh; Abbot of St Edmund's and Rork from him; Roger d'Auberville; Hugh de Montfort; Ranulph Peverel; Berard from Robert FitzCorbucion. Church.* ⊞ Attractive; pottery. The clay here has attracted potters since Roman days; 25 Roman kilns were found nearby.

Wilton Wiltshire: *Hervey of Wilton; William d'Eu; Hugh FitzBaldric.* Town, famous in the Middle Ages for its many religious houses (12 parish churches). Carpets were first made here in the 17th century. Wilton House and Park, seat of the Earls of Pembroke, was built in 1545, on the site of a 9th-century nunnery.

WEST WYCOMBE: *Row of cottages, 15th to 18th c.*

West Wycombe
Buckinghamshire: *Bishop of Winchester; Roger from Bishop of Bayeux; William from Count of Mortain. 3 mills, fishery at 1000 eels.* ⊞ Home of Sir Francis Dashwood (1708–81) who founded the Knights of St Francis of Wycombe.

Wadsworth West Riding, Yorkshire: *King's land. 2 churches.* Moorland area with scattered houses. An isolated building at Top Withins is said to be the setting for Emily Brontë's *Wuthering Heights* (1847).

Walton (near Glastonbury) Somerset: *Glastonbury Church. 10 cattle.* ⌂ Thatched 15th-century rectory.

West Bridgford Nottinghamshire: *William Peverel.* Town adjoining Nottingham, mentioned in *The Anglo-Saxon Chronicles* for the year 920, when Edward the Elder ordered a bridge across the Trent.

Winfarthing Norfolk: *King's land, in the custody of Godric. 2 horses at the hall.* ⌂ Famous for the Sword of Winfarthing, reputedly left by a thief who sheltered in the churchyard, and enshrined later in the church. It was said to help find lost objects, and lose unwanted husbands, although the sword was itself lost.

Witham Friary Somerset: *William from Roger de Courseulles.* ⌂ Ruins of England's first Carthusian monastery, founded by Henry II in penance for Becket's murder, near Witham Farm Hall. The church, c.1200, was restored in the 19th century.

Wilmcote Warwickshire: *Urso from Osbern FitzRichard.* ⌂ Mary Arden's House.

WILMCOTE: *Mary Arden's home as a girl.*

Whitchurch Devonshire: *Roald Dubbed.* ⌂ 2 old crosses mark the Abbot's Way from Tavistock. Honour Oak, on the Tavistock road, was the parole boundary for French prisoners of war from Princetown, during the Napoleonic wars.

West Tarring Sussex: *Archbishop of Canterbury; William de Braose. 2 churches.* Part of Worthing; some old buildings. Thomas à Becket is said to have introduced the fig into his garden here.

WORCESTER: *The gateway to the cathedral green.*

Worcester Worcestershire: *Worcester Church, and Urso, Osbern FitzRichard, Walter Ponther and Robert the Bursar from the church; Evesham Church.* City on the River Severn. The cathedral, rebuilt by Bishop Wulfstan, c. 1080, has an 11th-century crypt, Norman cloisters and a Norman chapter house.

Wormingford Essex: *Ilger from Robert Gernon. Mill, fishery, 7 beehives. 33 cattle, 200 sheep, 47 goats.* Hundreds of Roman urns were discovered here in the 19th century.

Williton Somerset: *King's land. Assessed with Cannington, etc.* Birthplace of Reginald Fitzurse, one of Thomas à Becket's murderers.

Watchet Somerset: *Dodman from William de Mohun. Mill.* Small port, a paper-making centre since the 17th century. Coleridge's 'ancient mariner' set sail from here.

Warboys Huntingdonshire: *Ramsey Abbey. Church.* Fenland. After the deaths of the witches of Warboys in 1593, Henry Cromwell, Oliver's son, paid a Cambridge lecturer to preach against witchcraft each year in Huntingdon, a custom that continued until 1814.

Wem Shropshire: *William Pantulf from Earl Roger. Falcon's eyrie, enclosed hunting wood.* Small market town. The notorious Judge Jeffreys was sold the barony of Wem, 1685.

Weston under Penyard Herefordshire: *Bernard from Durand of Gloucester.* Stone-built; castle remains. The site of the Roman settlement of *Ariconium* is nearby.

Wakefield West Riding, Yorkshire: *King's land. 2 churches.* County town and cathedral city. Industries include coal-mining, textiles, brewing, and engineering. Its cathedral has Norman traces and the tallest crocketed spire in Yorkshire (247 ft.); famous cycle of Mystery Plays.

Woodspring Somerset: *William de Falaise (given to him by Serlo de Burcy when he married Serlo's daughter).* Woodspring Priory, founded c.1200 by the grandson of Reginald Fitzurse, one of Thomas à Becket's murderers; recently restored.

Waterbeach Cambridgeshire: *Mucel from Picot of Cambridge; 2 of the king's carpenters.* Large. Denny Abbey, originally a Benedictine monastery, later housed the Knights Templar; after them, Franciscan nuns.

Weston Turville Buckinghamshire: *Bishop of Lisieux and Roger from Bishop of Bayeux. 4 mills.* The 18th-century manor house is in the outer bailey of a Norman castle, near a moat and motte.

WESTON TURVILLE: *Double-entry lych-gate.*

Wymondham Norfolk: *King's land, in the charge of William de Noyers; William de Warenne. 2 mills, fishery. 2 cobs, 16 cattle, 50 pigs, 24 sheep.* Small town with a half-timbered cross in its market square. A priory, now ruined, was established by the Benedictines of St Albans in 1207.

WYMONDHAM: *In winter the abbey's tall towers suggest something of its violent history.*

Richard FitzGilbert holds YALDING. Aethelred held it from King Edward. It answered for 2 sulungs then and now.... 16 villagers with 12 smallholders have 6 ploughs. 2 churches; 15 slaves; 2 mills at 25s; 4 fisheries at 1700 eels less 20. Meadow ... woodland, 150 pigs. Value before 1066 and later £30; now £20, because the land has been despoiled of livestock.

Yalding is one of the county's prettiest villages. Here the River Beult (pronounced Belt) is crossed by a long medieval bridge. The river periodically floods, hence the steps which lead up to the front doors of many of the cottages. Perhaps some disastrous flood explains *Domesday*'s note that Yalding had no livestock.

Richard FitzGilbert was an opportunist, insufficiently astute always to back the winning side. When William I died he joined Odo, Bishop of Bayeux, in support of Robert of Normandy's claim to succeed instead of William Rufus. They lost and Richard was imprisoned and died.

Throughout the Middle Ages Yalding had been a rustic settlement until hops brought it prosperity. Then each summer ever-increasing numbers of pickers from the east end of London would arrive for their annual working holiday. In the 1870s a great fight was staged between a picker, 'The Booster', and a gypsy, 'Billy Slit Nose'. When four policemen forced their way through the crowd of 2000, the fighters knocked them to the ground; the ensuing riot left the road looking 'more like a slaughter house than a village street'.

Eels are still caught at Yalding, as they were in 1086, though not in such quantity, and none to compare with the monster landed in 1757. It was 5 feet 9 inches long, 18 inches in girth, and weighed 40 pounds – a worthy dish for Richard FitzGilbert.

YORK: *An old wall safe in All Saint's church.*

York North Riding, Yorkshire: *King's land; Archbishop of York before and after 1066; numerous other holders and burgesses. Churches, castle, many dwellings.* City and archiepiscopal see. University; racecourse; industries include chocolate (established by the Quaker families of Rowntree and Terry. The medieval city walls are largely intact and the Shambles is possibly the finest medieval street in Europe. St Peter's School, which claims to be the oldest in Britain, forbids bonfires as Guy Fawkes was a pupil.

Yealmpton Devonshire: *King's land and the clergy of this village from the king.* 🏠 Sarah Martin wrote 'Old Mother Hubbard', based on the housekeeper, in Kitley House. Bones of prehistoric animals were found in a cave at Yealmbridge.

Yeovil Somerset: *Count of Mortain and Amund from him; Hugh from William d'Eu. 2 mills.* Market town, known for glove-making since the 18th century; industries now include helicopter manufacture.

Yelling Huntingdonshire: *Swein from Ramsey Abbey. Aubrey de Vere. Church.* 🏠 Quiet. Italian paintings in the late Norman church were part of Napoleon's loot, and bought by a private collector.

Yoxford Suffolk: *Roger Bigot and Ayleward the king's reeve from him; Roger de Tosny.* 🏠 Called 'the garden of Suffolk'. The village street was once a Roman road.

Yate Gloucestershire: *Bishop of Worcester.* Overspill town for Bristol and Bath. A stone called Celestine, used in purifying sugar, is found here.

Yattendon Berkshire: *Godbald from William FitzAnsculf. Mill.* 🏠 Once a market town; attractive cottages. Bronze Age implements (The Yattendon Hoard) were found here.

Yelford Oxfordshire: *Walter Poyntz.* 🏠 Family home of Warren Hastings, governor-general of India (1773–85).

Yarm North Riding, Yorkshire: *King's land.* Town in a loop of the River Tees; almost an island, which makes it liable to flooding; many Georgian buildings; a meeting at the George and Dragon Inn in 1820 planned the first public railway – from Stockton to Darlington.

Youlgreave Derbyshire: *Henry de Ferrers. Mill.* 🏠 Name is a corruption of the Saxon 'auldgroove', meaning old mine. Well-dressing displays and a carnival are held in July.

Yazor Herefordshire: *Robert from Roger de Lacy.* 🏠 House of Sir Uvedale Price, 19th-century theorist of the English Picturesque.

YARPOLE: *The old bakehouse.*

Yarpole Herefordshire: *King's land; Leofwin Latimer; Robert Gernon.* 🏠

Zeal Monachorum Devonshire: *Buckfast Church.* 🏠 Given by King Canute to the monks of Buckfast Church. A block of stone in the churchyard is possibly the altar of the Norman church.

Zeals Wiltshire: *Jocelyn Rivers; Alfgeat from the king. 2 mills.* 🏠 Charles II hid in Zeals House when fleeing Cromwell's men in 1651.

YALDING: *View of hopfields and oast-houses.*

Index

Acknowledgements

Cover Design: Anthony Short
Maps and drawings: Dennis Curran
Photographs:
   Public Records Office: pages 2, 5, 7
   British Tourist Authority: 32, 36, 48, 57, 72, 76–77, 80, 87
   all others: Marianne Majerus